MW00614432

FAITH HEALING

INSIGHTS FROM ETHAN OTIS ALLEN, THE FIRST AMERICAN HEALING EVANGELIST

ETHAN OTIS ALLEN

Edited by

J.D. KING

Foreword by

JENNIFER A. MISKOV

Christos

Faith Healing: Insights from Ethan Allen, the First American Healing Evangelist
Copyright © 2020 by Christos Publishing
P.O. Box 1333
Lee's Summit, Missouri 64063

ISBN: 978-1-950053-33-9

The image of Ethan Otis Allen was used by permission of the *Flower Pentecostal Center* in Springfield, Missouri.

This book includes material originally published in the following public domain works:

-Allen, Ethan Otis, *Faith Healing: What I Have Witnessed of the Fulfillment of James 5:14–16* (Philadelphia: G. W. McCalla, 1881).

-MacArthur, William T., "Ethan Allen" (Philadelphia: Office of the Parlor Evangelist, undated [1924?]).

-Reiff, Anna C., "Miracles Wrought Through Prayer and Fasting: The Story of a Man who Walked with God," *Latter Rain Evangel* 22:8 (May 1930), 6-8.

This book is not intended as a substitute for the advice of licensed medical professionals. The reader should regularly consult a physician in matters relating to his or her health and particularly with respect to any symptoms that may require diagnosis or medical attention.

Christos Publishing produces superbly researched Christian books informed by a Spirit-led worldview.

"Let Christ make you the ministers of His healing as well as sin-destroying power, for Christ both healed and forgave sins at the same time. Now, why hold to the one and neglect the other? Why set one lamp on the stand and the other under the bushel?"

—ETHAN OTIS ALLEN

CONTENTS

ACKNOWLEDGMENTS

A book worth reading is seldom brought to life in solitude. More often than not, it is the product of a benevolent and engaged community. That is undoubtedly true of *Faith Healing: Insights from Ethan Otis Allen, the First American Healing Evangelist.*

First of all, I wish to acknowledge Carole Hawkins, Esther Tsai, and Phyllis Demeo for your editorial assistance. You helped disentangle a badly jumbled text. Thank you!

I also want to celebrate the elegant layout and design of Rachel Greene. Manuscripts always seem to come alive with your capable touch.

Shawn Jonas, you somehow forged a magnificent cover out of an old, tattered photograph. You achieved something that I thought was nearly impossible.

In highlighting the generosity that I have received, I also want to thank Pastors Steve and Kathy Gray—along with World Revival Church in Kansas City, Missouri. This extraordinary spiritual community has been beside me along the way, providing endless support and encouragement.

Finally, I could accomplish nothing without the backing of my wonderful wife and kids. Bobbie, my greatest love, you offer unending patience and affection. I am overwhelmed by you. Allyson and Matthew, thank you for giving your father the opportunities to reflect and write. My family is, perhaps, the greatest gift of all.

FOREWORD

JENNIFER A. MISKOV, PH.D.

I am so thankful for J.D. King stewarding this important
and forgotten story, giving honor where honor is due.
Ethan Otis Allen was such a significant pioneer of
pioneers. Never seeking a platform, he would go out to
many who would normally be overlooked or forgotten so
that he could demonstrate the love and power of God.

He was a forerunner in the Divine Healing
Movement, teaching and modeling the power to heal
before it was accepted in the church. Allen's passion for
healing paved the way for other prominent healing
evangelists to come after him. He influenced many other
influencers, much of the time humbly from behind the
scenes. Even though Allen was shy and more
introverted, that didn't stop God from raising him up as
a father in the Faith Cure movement.

Allen was determined to set people free and see them

delivered from sickness no matter how long it took. He took the time to travel just to pray for the one God called him to pray for, many times fasting until he was able to see the full deliverance.

He was known as a father in the faith to many. His life brings hope and faith to us all. His story now told shows that God can use any individual who gives his or her wholehearted yes to Him.

I know I am personally indebted to Ethan Otis Allen's yes to God. If it wasn't for him, I might not be where I am at today. He had the courage to pray for African American Sarah Ann Freeman Mix during a time racial segregation and long before the Civil Rights movement came to the scene. Because of his courage to cross the racial divide to demonstrate the love of God, Sarah was radically healed. Not only that, Allen even invited Sarah and her husband Edward to travel and minister together with him afterwards.

Following her healing, Sarah's testimony got printed in a newspaper. This article came to the attention of Carrie Judd Montgomery's family in Buffalo, New York. They were desperate for Carrie's healing and had already lost several of their other children to sickness. When things look the darkest, they read Sarah's testimony in the public newspaper about how she was healed when Allen prayed for her. They immediately wrote to Mrs. Mix, as she was commonly referred to, asking her to pray for Carrie. Mrs. Mix quickly responded with a letter to Carrie encouraging her to set aside time on February

26, 1879, to pray between 3:00-4:00 pm and then to act in faith according to God's Word found in James 5. Mrs. Mix who was in Connecticut, had a prayer meeting at that time and agreed to pray long distance for Carrie. Then during that set apart time of prayer, around 3:30 pm and while on her death bed, Carrie was miraculously healed by the power of God and in answer to the prayers of Mrs. Mix. Carrie later went on to have a very significant healing ministry.

I later discovered Carrie Judd Montgomery when I was doing my Ph.D. while in England. I was so captivated and inspired by her faith in God, that I decided to do my whole Ph.D. thesis on her life and theology. Carrie's life and testimonies have given me the courage and strength to step into some of my own breakthroughs. Discovering her story has literally shifted the trajectory of my life in a powerful direction for which I am so blessed. None of this would have happened without Allen's one yes.

The momentum of one yes is so powerful. From Ethan Otis Allen's one yes to cross over racial divides to love the one in front of him, to Mrs. Mix's yes to pray for Carrie in her time of desperate need, from Carrie's yes to open up some of the earliest healing homes in the nation, to my yes, inspired by Carrie's faith, to step out and plant a revival community around God's presence, the momentum continues to build. The question I want to ask us today is, what are we going to do with the momentum that Ethan Otis Allen began with his one yes? How will we take the ground that he's paved for us and go even further in our day?

—Jennifer A. Miskov, Ph.D., author of *Life on Wings: The Forgotten Life and Theology of Carrie Judd Montgomery* (1858-1946)

INTRODUCTION

J. D. KING

The motivation for this work goes back nearly twenty-five years. While plumbing the depths of Pentecostalism and seeking to discover something about my upbringing, I learned of an adjacent healing revival. I recall being astonished by the marvelous tales. At the time, I didn't know much about the Faith Cure Movement, but I was intrigued by a few of the leading figures and their extraordinary encounters.

In the 1880s and 90s, this transatlantic awakening touched thousands of lives and set the stage for global Pentecostalism.[1] Crippled people deserted their crutches —walking for the first time in years. The formerly bedridden were regaining vitality. Miracles flourished.

In this revival, outstanding figures emerged. The afflicted masses heard from anointed preachers like A. B. Simpson (1843-1919), Carrie Judd Montgomery (1858-1946), John Alexander Dowie (1847-1907), and Maria

Woodworth-Etter (1844-1924). These exceptional men and women brought the message of divine healing to the forefront.

But in probing the Faith Cure Movement, I observed lesser-known figures that also made significant contributions—Charles Cullis (1833-1892), W. E. Boardman (1810-1886), and Sarah Ann Freeman Mix (1832-1884).

One name, however, stood out in my studies—Ethan Otis Allen (1813-1903). I read stories about this penniless man and how he launched the ministry of healing, alone, in the United States in the 1840s. I found his mysterious life captivating.

A few years afterward, I came into possession of an old, beat-up copy of Allen's book, *Faith Healing: Or What I Have Witnessed of the Fulfillment of James 5:14–16*. After poring over it, I felt it would be good to make this forgotten work accessible to others.

I put this proposal on hold for several years. Eventually, I got around to editing an assortment of Ethan Allen material. This particular work is what you're now holding in your hands.

I have organized this inspirational book into three sections. The first is a biographical sketch of Ethan O. Allen. The second is a modern edition of Allen's *Faith Healing*. The last segment is a compilation of testimonies and personal musings from colleagues and friends.

In the first portion of this text, I wanted to create a biographical sketch, along with a brief introduction to

Allen's theology and practices. This section aims to introduce this marvelous intercessor's life. The heart of this book is, however, located in the second segment. It includes Allen's *Faith Healing: Or What I Have Witnessed of the Fulfillment of James 5:14–16*. Here, the evangelist's interpretations and observations are available for direct examination. This material is an absolute treasure.

The last part of this publication includes impressions from figures that had direct contact with Allen's ministry. This section provides valued insights about this neglected spiritual father.

This book intends to reassert the magnificent legacy of healing in America and remind believers how God uses the unlikely. I hope that you're inspired by *Faith Healing: Insights from Ethan Otis Allen, the First American Healing Evangelist*.

—J. D. King
Christos Publishing

"Now, Lord, help us to get our fingers around this grain of mustard seed."

—Ethan O. Allen

FORGOTTEN FATHER

THE FIRST AMERICAN HEALING EVANGELIST

J.D. KING

G od has chosen the weak things of the world to confound the wise" (1 Cor. 1:27). In a society obsessed with affluence, God turns things on its head, utilizing the poor and marginalized.

The story of Ethan Otis Allen (1813–1903) shows this pattern. This impoverished laborer pioneered modern healing practices, setting the stage for the American Faith Cure Movement (1880–1900)[1] and Pentecostalism (1901–1946).[2]

A. B. Simpson (1843-1919), the founder of the Christian and Missionary Alliance, deemed Allen the "Father of Divine Healing in America."[3] But this man, who opened the door to such a remarkable dimension of the Kingdom, has been mostly forgotten. Allen's magnificent story deserves a fresh retelling.

CHILDHOOD AND SICKNESS

Ethan Otis Allen breathed his first breath on a small family farm in Belchertown, Massachusetts, on August 25, 1813. He was one of six children born to Joel and Lydia Allen, penniless farmers.

Allen was scarcely six years of age when his father died. This tragedy left his family reeling. Unschooled and devoid of social refinement, Allen remained destitute most of his life.

Allen contracted pulmonary tuberculosis—damaging his liver and other parts of his body. This diagnosis was a virtual death sentence. Hampered by his frailty and slight build, hard labor was an impossibility. Allen had to settle for employment at the poorhouse[4] in Westfield, Massachusetts.

Impoverished and hindered by a sickness that "continued to undermine his health,"[5] it looked as though Allen's life was going nowhere.

HEALED OF PULMONARY TUBERCULOSIS

Allen felt curiously attracted to an evening church service at a country schoolhouse in 1846. The Methodists, who organized the meeting, were once zealous revivalists, but the zeal had waned.[6] Yet, not everything was lost.

Although the night was dreary, souls were in the balance. The Methodists wanted all the farmers and laborers to know God. By the conclusion of the service, one evangelist asked Allen if he wanted to deepen his faith commitment. Inexplicably stirred, Allen sought the Lord.

A jubilant Allen asked if the leaders would address an added concern. He said, "Brethren, if you will pray for me, I believe that this mighty power that has come upon me will heal my lung."[7]

The party felt this was a peculiar request. Although John Wesley (1703-1792) and his itinerates had prayerfully sought cures for the sick in the eighteenth and early nineteenth centuries,[8] it was less common for Methodists to deal with disease in 1846.

Nevertheless, one of the Methodists was reminded of what Jesus proclaimed in Mark 16:18: "They shall lay hands on the sick, and they shall recover." He said, "Let's try it." There wasn't much intensity, but as the team concluded their prayers, Allen was "instantly and perfectly healed."[9]

THE BEGINNING OF HIS MINISTRY

This infusion of grace revolutionized Allen's life. He discovered his life purpose. Coming back to the Westfield poorhouse, Allen humbly interceded for the households under his care. The power of Jesus Christ rescued several who were struggling with mental and physical disorders.

Allen became captivated by the beauty of intercession and spent extended hours communing with

God. This frail, poorhouse manager became recognized as "a man of faith."[10]

Ignoring his low estate and lack of education, Allen courageously prayed for the indigent, sick, and feeble-minded. William MacArthur writes

He was so childlike that one was driven to the conclusion that therein lay the secret of his success. His heart was so simple that he seemed to expect the Lord to do whatsoever he asked, and he was not disappointed.[11]

Under the Spirit's leadings, Allen interceded for not only individuals close to home but also those at considerable distances. It was typical "for him to travel hundreds of miles to pray individually with one person."[12]

Allen continued laboring with the poor for a few more years but began focusing more of his time on the healing ministry. Invitations took him into "poor houses where he prayed not only for the improvident and the incurable but also the epileptics and the insane."[13] Occasionally Allen spoke in small churches, where his blunt talk was not always appreciated.

Unsurprisingly, Allen sensed a divine calling on his life. The words of Luke 10:19 leaped out: "Behold, I give unto you power to tread on serpents and scorpions, and over all the power of the enemy: and nothing shall by any means hurt you."

Although loosely identifying with Methodism, Allen did not feel wholly at home in their ranks.[14] Rough and unschooled, many doubted the capabilities of a poorhouse manager. So, he started his ministry alone—unaffiliated and unaccredited.[15]

SUPERNATURALISTIC APPROACH TO HEALING

Not having anyone with which to align until the 1870s, Allen had to forge a lonely path for twenty-five years. He would later say that his "only teacher was the Spirit of God; his only textbook was the Bible."[16]

Few in antebellum America approached healing like Allen. It wasn't unusual for Christians to pray for improved health, but he welded a "waring charismaticism."[17] Allen unapologetically rooted his endeavors in the miraculous—apparently not educated enough to know that he wasn't supposed to.

As Allen pioneered a supernaturalistic approach in America, a comparable ideology was developing across the Atlantic. Johann Christoph Blumhardt (1805-1880) of Germany[18] and Dorothea Trudel (1813-1862) of Switzerland[19] were also laying claim to vibrant New Testament healings.[20]

By the late nineteenth century, divine healing was experienced on a broader scale in North America and Europe. Many began praying for the sick as they anticipated a fresh outpouring of the Holy Spirit. In many ways, Ethan Otis Allen was the harbinger of this awakening in the United States.

NOT DEPENDING ON THE FLESH

Unmotivated by anything from the "flesh" (Gal. 5:16-17),[21] Allen was selective about who he prayed for. He would only intercede for individuals that God led him to. In one occurrence, Allen refused to pray for his own grandchild because he had no sense of release. He "always endeavored to ascertain if there was any hindrance, and if there was, he would not pray for healing."[22]

Fasting was also a vital part of Allen's regimen. It was common for him to go without food for several days. He recognized that this discipline was crucial for triumphing over severe diseases (Matt. 17:21).

Many times, Allen "insisted on fasting by the side of the sick person. An associated minister said that "he once knew him to refuse both food and water for six days and nights."[23]

In extraordinary illnesses, Allen insisted that a near relative accompany him in a fast. He would expect this family member to abstain from food as long as he did. In the Bible, Allen noticed that when "dealing with children and irresponsible adults," Jesus always "acted in conjunction with parents or near relatives."[24] He always felt that it was wise to follow the same pattern. The principles of the Kingdom of God never change.

Allen only moved when he saw God move. Neither prestige nor wealth motivated him. He didn't care if anyone knew who he was or what he accomplished.

Allen's only concern was pleasing the Lord and extending the reach of heaven's dominion.

ALLEN'S METHODOLOGY OF HEALING

When Allen visited an afflicted man or woman, he "never anointed . . . with oil, nor did he claim to be an elder of the Church. Rather, he simply claimed the biblical promise given to 'them that believe' (Mark 16:17)."[25]

With little fanfare, Allen would usually begin the healing process with fasting and reviewing relevant biblical passages to prepare the recipient's heart for the breakthrough. His approach

> was usually one-on-one, which enabled him to spend several days with a patient if necessary, explaining to him the biblical basis of healing and helping to strengthen his faith and expectation that God was going to heal him now.[26]

After establishing a firm scriptural foundation, Allen would ask a string of questions: "Do you believe that the Lord is able to heal you?" "Do you believe that he is willing to heal you?" "Do you believe that he wants to do it now?"[27] If the recipient could not say "yes" to each question, Allen knew more preparations were necessary.

Allen maintained that "expectation was an essential element in receiving healing. The sick needed to believe, visualize, and expect that God would do whatever they asked of Him in faith."[28] Without a sense of expectation, there was no reason to pray.[29]

As soon as Allen observed a sign of faith from the sufferer, he would profess the following from Mark 16:17-18: "And these signs shall follow them that believe; In my name, they shall . . . lay hands on the sick, and they shall recover."[30]

Afterward, Allen placed his hand on this sick person and uttered bold, commanding prayers. He used intercession like a weapon against the hellish afflictions of the enemy.[31]

Whenever Allen interceded for an individual, he thought something would happen instantaneously. This rough evangelist "expected the healing to come then and there, and if it did not, he simply renewed his efforts."[32]

Allen always continued in prayer until he felt the burden of intercession lift. Virtually every "healing was approached with unhurried forbearance."[33]

Describing some of what he witnessed while alongside Allen in his healing missions, Edgar Sellew shared the following:

> He was settled in his convictions and would not go to any call until he had waited before the Lord for the Holy Spirit to witness to the call as being from God. He was in the habit of much fasting before the Lord; then when the Lord spoke in his heart, nothing was allowed to swerve him from the course he thought was God's ordering. He would not take the difficult case until he had fasted, and, in many cases, he insisted on

fasting by the one who was sick . . . He was very
modest in manner, and he never pushed his views
forward but was always ready to give a reason for the
hope set within him. He was more simple, sane, and
scriptural on the subject of healing than any other
person I ever met.[34]

Although a tender, soft-spoken man, Allen was fierce
in his underlying technique. Naturally, his aggressive
tone was not always welcomed. Allen knew that "he was
the subject of adverse criticism." But the fact that "the
sick were actually healed in answer to his prayers
encouraged him to press on."[35]

Not easily deterred, Allen often declared, "I'm
believin' and receivin' . . . Praise God, I'm believin' and
receivin.'" One of his friends conceded that he had never
"known him to ask for anything that he did not
receive."[36]

SPIRITUALLY ROOTED DISEASES

To Allen, "the physical and spiritual were inseparable in
regard to disease." Any physical infirmity, no matter
how it appeared, was spiritually rooted. In his
understanding, "all sickness was either directly or
indirectly the work of Satan."

To counteract "the physical problem, one first had to
defeat the spiritual problem." So, Allen engaged in the
"practice of rebuking—or 'casting out' as he termed it—
the evil spirit before he prayed for the sick one."

Physical healing necessitated "a confrontation with Satan and his demonic forces."[37]

Providing a glimpse into Allen's mindset, MacArthur shared the following:

> It was inspiring as well as instructive to hear him talk—first to the devil, then to the Lord, and lastly to the sick person. To the devil, he would sometimes say, "Oh, yes, you have had a fine time, haven't you? Yes, a fine time, but I am here now, and I am going to put the name of Jesus on you, and you can't stand that!" Then he would turn and say so reverently, "Blessed Jesus, you know me. You know that I stand on the 'Old Commission'" (meaning Mark 16:17–18). Then he would turn to the sick one and say, "Now I am going to heal you in the name of Jesus."[38]

A specific example of Allen's supernaturalistic approach is recorded in the *Galveston Daily News* on October 5, 1884.

A destitute man from Detroit was dying of tuberculosis and asked the evangelist to travel and pray for him. When Allen made the journey from Massachusetts, the interchange went as follows:

> "This kind goeth not out but by prayer and fasting," and thereupon began a three-day fast. At the end of the three days, he prayed . . . [The man] was cured, but by a remarkable process. He was seized with a terrible fit

of bilious vomiting, after which he rapidly recovered his health, and is a well man today.[39]

Allen believed that it was the responsibility of "the Church to appropriate the victory of Christ over Satan."[40] He wasn't fearful of the forces of darkness. Evil will never prevail over God's holy Church.

TESTIMONIES OF HEALING

Testimonies of healing frequently accompanied Ethan Allen's ministry. One individual that he prayed for was Thomas Gross, a Methodist from a respected family. Gross had found himself "reduced to a mere wreck of a man by mental derangement." Allen cared for him in the poorhouse and compassionately interceded for him. They recorded the following testimony:

I felt encouraged by the spirit of faith and prayer. . . I followed up the prayer till God took away all burdens, and I felt the blessed assurance that God was working. Immediately after, I discovered his mind beginning to return.[41]

Another remarkable account is the healing of Sarah Minot Chase Musgrove (1839–1933). She came down with a debilitating illness and was bedridden for four years. Musgrove had consulted several doctors, but they were powerless to help her. She was not expected to live much longer.

In January 1882, reaching a point of desperation, she journeyed to the Women's Faith Home for Incurables, a healing home in Brooklyn, New York. Some workers asked Allen if he would come and pray. He sought the Lord and felt he was supposed to go.

Musgrove recounted the following:

So, obediently, Allen took the journey from Springfield, Massachusetts, to Brooklyn, New York. Arriving at the home about supper time, he was asked to eat his supper before praying with me. His reply was characteristic of this humble, obedient servant of the Lord: "No. The Lord has important work for me in this home; I shall neither eat nor drink until it is accomplished." Then, coming at once to me, very quietly, he asked regarding my Christian experience and offered a simple prayer, like a little child to its father, asking that God would verify His own Word. Turning to me, he asked, "Do you believe that the Lord is able to heal you?"

"Yes."

"That He is willing to?"

"Yes."

"That He wants to do it now?"

"Yes."

Then repeating the words "They that believe shall lay hands on the sick, and they shall recover," he laid his hands upon me in the name of Jesus and told the Lord that he believed, on the authority of His Word, that I was healed. I also believed it, and together, we praised the Lord for healing me, new life thrilled and thrilled through my entire being. The forty-two years since that hour have proved the healing permanent.[42]

After Musgrove was healed, she interceded for the sick as well. Allen talked her into opening a faith healing home in Troy, New York, in 1883. It was an outreach that she faithfully continued for several decades.[43] Forty-year-old Sarah Musgrove was given a death sentence, but because of Jesus' healing virtue, she "lived in full vigor till her ninety-fifth year."[44]

Another remarkable healing was narrated in the pages of *The Christian and Missionary Alliance Magazine*. The thirteen-year-old son of Seth (1854-1933) and Hulda Rees (1855-1898) of Providence, Rhode Island, had acute nephritis, a kidney disease. The family reached out to Allen, and he trekked hundreds of miles to intercede for the boy.

Although it was then late at night and he was an old man of eighty-two years of age, he boarded a late train, . . . reaching our home in Providence a few minutes before midnight. As he stepped into the house entirely unaccompanied and a perfect stranger to us, he said, "I am sent as was Peter to the house of Cornelius, your prayers are heard and are to be answered." He asked if there was any unbelief in the house, and was assured there was none . . . He then laid his hands on the child in the name of Jesus and prayed with wonderful power and faith. The glory of the Lord came down and flooded the room. He rebuked the disease in the name of Jesus and commanded the devil to depart. While he was yet praying, the fever began to abate, and the child's skin became moist, and from that hour, the fever left him. He was left very weak, but consciousness soon returned, and he roused and said he was hungry. Today he is well—gloriously healed.[45]

This experience deepened Rees' confidence in the certainty of divine healing. Allen influenced several of the leading Holiness stalwarts in the late 1800s. People change the world in ways difficult to quantify.

Later, in the pages of *The Latter Rain Evangel*, there was an account of a poisoned man with a horrendously swollen body. He was healed under the gracious efforts of Allen.

There was one case of a man who had been poisoned and was badly swollen. "Father Allen," as he was familiarly known, had a great deal to say to the devil on this occasion, praying for every part of the man's body except his feet. The next day the man returned well, the swelling completely gone except from his feet. "Father Allen" was deeply stirred. "There," he said, "you see when you partic'larize you've got to be partic'lar! I never said a word about them feet." Then turning on the devil, he said, "Oh yes, you thought because I never mentioned them feet that you'd just stay there. In the name of Jesus, come out!" The feet became normal almost immediately.[46]

Allen understood the power of concentrated prayer.

When an intercessor's prayers are not focused, they lack impact. This was a crucial matter to Allen.

Another striking testimony was depicted in Carrie Judd Montgomery's *Triumphs of Faith Journal*. The account describes what happened to a disabled man as Allen prayed for him:

> As Mr. Allen offered prayer, laying his hands upon me in the name of the Lord, I felt an intense heat and moisture over the surface of my body, until at length, my whole being was permeated by this divine healing power, and I unhesitatingly declared myself healed. Then rising, in the name of the Lord, I walked several times across the floor. I was freed from all the pain, and like the nobleman's son, began to mend from that very hour.[47]

Allen occasionally witnessed heat, trembling, and other unusual sensations when he interceded for the sick. These were merely outward signs of an invisible, spiritual work.

The marvelous work that Ethan Allen conducted over several decades was undocumented. Never prone to self-promotion, his healing encounters were never compiled. Allen even downplayed the miracle stories in his writing.[48] This weathered intercessor wanted glory for Jesus, not himself.

TRAVELING COMPANIONS

Although Allen tied the cures to "the gift of healing,"[49] he didn't believe that grace was exclusive. The evangelist believed that ordinary Christians could also operate in works of power.

The ministry of healing wasn't reserved for bureaucrats or pastors; it was a dynamic act of faith for anyone who loved Jesus. Drawing insights from Genesis 3:15 and Luke 10:19, Allen insisted every Christian had authority over Satan, the author of disease.

In a tract titled, "Satan Under Your Feet," Allen makes a threefold argument for this assertion.

> First, Christ put Satan's head under His feet at Calvary, thus bruising him. Second, Christ has given to every believer the right to tread on Satan's head and to bruise him. Third, God has promised each believer the power to subdue Satan if he will simply appropriate by faith the victory of Christ on the cross.[50]

Allen wanted to train up others for ministry, so he often brought "traveling companions as he visited the sick and suffering."[51] In the 1860s, he worked alongside Charles Bush, a lay intercessor in Oakfield, Wisconsin. Another strategic partner was Allen's "intimate and lifelong friend,"[52] Edgar K. Sellew (1840-1915) of East Long Meadow, Massachusetts.

William Telfer MacArthur (1861-1949), a preacher affiliated with A. B. Simpson and the Christian and

Missionary Alliance, ministered alongside Allen in his later years.

Allen also partnered with Sarah M. C. Musgrove (1839-1933) of Troy, New York, and Mary Shoemaker (1846-1916), a gifted intercessor from Springfield, Massachusetts. Both women had dynamic healing ministries in their own right.

Perhaps Allen's most vital associate was Sarah Ann Freeman Mix (1832-1884), a "well-educated, articulate, and persuasive"[53] African-American from Wolcottville, Connecticut. She was healed of tuberculosis on December 19, 1877, after Allen interceded. Mix reminisced,

> I was healed by faith and prayer and the laying on of hands by Brother Ethan O. Allen, of Springfield, Massachusetts, one who has the gift of healing. The Lord works mightily through him. And God in His goodness and mercy has blessed me with this blessed boon, the gift of faith, and the healing by the laying on of hands and the prayer of faith. How many, God only knows, have been benefited through unworthy me. Eternity itself can only reveal the numbers.[54]

Allen told Mix that she "had the power of healing in her,"[55] and she was later recruited to serve alongside him in ministry.[56] Sarah and her husband, Edward, "traveled with Allen until they decided to devote full time to their own independent faith healing ministry."[57] Mix ministered to over 230 people over the next seven

years. The most noted of which was Carrie Judd
Montgomery (1858-1946) of Buffalo, New York.

When contemplating the intercessors and evangelists
that Allen worked with, it is clear that he left an
extraordinary spiritual heritage. A father's greatest
legacy is always his sons and daughters.

THE FRUITS OF HIS MINISTRY

Despite his tendency to move along the periphery, Allen
was tremendously fruitful. Along with other efforts, he
assisted Mary Shoemaker (1846-1916) in the founding
of Shiloh Chapel, a healing home in Springfield,
Massachusetts. This was a facility that the sick could
visit to find rest, scriptural teaching, and personal
prayer. In the 1880s and 90s, several of these facilities
were being established across the United States.[58]

Allen spent fifty years traveling "New England and
the eastern half of the United States, praying for the sick
and teaching divine healing."[59] In these journeys, he was
able to minister in most of the burgeoning healing
homes.

Some facilities Allen frequented included: Sara
Musgrove's Four-fold Gospel Mission in Troy, New York,
and Carrie Judd's "Faith Rest Cottage" in Buffalo, New
York. The aging evangelist was also known to stop over
at Sarah G. Beck's Kemuel House in Germantown,
Pennsylvania, J. P. Kellogg's home in Utica, New York,
and Dora Dudley's faith home in Grand Rapids,
Michigan.

Allen loved ministering in each of the fledgling institutions. However, his favorites were still "Charles Cullis' Faith Cure Home in Boston and A. B. Simpson's Berachah Home in New York City."[60] He naturally preferred being where the action was.

Although Allen was busy ministering in the healing homes and other gatherings, he was never so preoccupied that he couldn't pray for those who knocked on his door. Allen was an unabashed servant to the destitute. He gave of himself regularly for their salvation and restoration.

MOVING OUT OF ANONYMITY

As the Faith Cure Movement expanded during the last two decades of the nineteenth century, Ethan Allen was considered a forerunner and patriarch.

Because of his "reserved temperament and humble background,"[61] Allen's receptivity had been "limited to the disinherited of society."[62] It wasn't just his socio-economic status or "unschooled ways" that kept him from "a larger audience," Allen also had a "shy personality."[63]

This old poorhouse master never carried the same social clout as Dr. Charles Cullis or A. B. Simpson.[64] But the affluent who might have once discounted the battered old evangelist sought his counsel in the later years.

In the 1880s and 90s, Allen latched onto a "more sophisticated audience in the camp meetings and conventions of both Charles Cullis and A. B. Simpson."[65] The cultured and well-heeled listened to a barely literate laborer share the inexplicable wonders of the Kingdom of God and loved it.

In 1881, Allen released a book that recounted a few biographical details, along with observations about divine healing.[66] This small publication was titled *Faith Healing: Or What I Have Witnessed of the Fulfillment of James 5:14–16.*

This old intercessor, "in his homespun way, anticipated much that became more theologically explicit in the writings of . . . Stockmayer, Simpson, and Gordon."[67] Allen often gruffly highlighted the correlation between healing and the forgiveness of sins.

Despite the uncultured accouterments, many appreciated the wisdom and theological insight of Allen. After decades of anonymity, the father of divine healing in America was given a measure of recognition and honor.

THE LAST DAYS OF A FORGOTTEN GIANT

Ethan Allen's beloved wife, Keziah, died in the fall of 1893, leaving Him alone after fifty-six years of marriage. Shortly after that, he moved to Los Angeles, California, to live with his son.

While residing out West, this eighty-six-year-old continued praying for the sick as often as possible. Allen acknowledged that he "loved the climate of this place but was never satisfied when not working for the Lord."[68]

Though "unable to undertake long journeys or to undergo long fasts,"[69] Allen held meetings in Carrie Judd Montgomery's Home for Peace and preached in Christian and Missionary Alliance services. Allen continued to labor wherever he could, and multitudes still testified of "being healed through his instrumentality."[70]

In his modest bungalow behind his son's home, Allen received visitors and readily ministered to them.

No matter who visited the home or what their business was, . . . they spoke in hushed tones, as though they felt they were on holy ground. And what wonder! Behind the draperies sat the silent figure of one who had cultivated an acquaintance with God, such as a few have ever known.[71]

While young, Allen was told that he would surely be dead by thirty. But because of the healing power of God, he made it almost to ninety. This unrelenting evangelist gathered his last breath on January 24, 1903, living the "most remarkable life."[72]

Writing about his passing, Allen's close friend, Edgar Sellew, mournfully declared, "Surely a man of God has fallen."[73] The old intercessor "was faithful in that which seemed small in the eyes of men, but which was really great in the eyes of God."[74]

Allen was the first American healing evangelist—an

unpolished pioneer that broke open the door for a multitude of intercessors. While largely unknown, this "John the Baptist figure"[75] made vital contributions to the growth and acceptance of divine healing in the United States.

"These promises are for God's children to lay hold of as readily as on any others. We are in a land of demons and of sicknesses, and these promises of casting out and healing by prayer and laying on of hands are available, even in these days of apostasy."

—ETHAN O. ALLEN

PRELIMINARY THOUGHTS

FAITH HEALING—WHAT I HAVE WITNESSED OF THE FULFILLMENT OF JAMES 5:14–16

J.D. KING

Ethan O. Allen's *Faith Healing: What I Have Witnessed of the Fulfillment of James 5:14–16* was originally published in Philadelphia in 1881. This long-lost work is an intimate account and apologetic from one of the original healing evangelists in America.

Textual evidence indicates that most of Allen's book was written before 1870. It reflects earlier modalities and foreshadows insights later expanded through his participation in the Faith-Cure Movement.[1] Although most of Allen's succeeding ideas are resident here in seed-form, he advanced in a more radicalized direction in the 1880s.[2]

Exploring Allen's *Faith Healing* may require patience from the reader. Though anointed, he wasn't well educated. One of Allen's subsequent biographers suggested that he was in the same class as the rough and tumble disciples. William MacArthur writes, "As to educational advantages, judged by his bad grammar, he was in the class with Peter and John."[3]

The original manuscript of Faith Healing displays the limited literary talents of this nineteenth-century evangelist. To bring it suitably back into print, editing was unavoidable. Contemporary readers expect proper paragraphing, sentence construction, and subheadings. Many can't stomach bloated and complicated textual renderings. Thus, the book has been modernized.

In all of the modifications, the objective was to enhance readability without altering voice. We wanted Allen's observations to be understandable to the twenty-first century reader and faithful to his original revelations.

The discoveries of spiritual fathers are substantial, especially those whose remarks have been overlooked with time. Contemporary believers should try to discover who these individuals were and what God disclosed to them.

Modern believers don't consistently recognize it, but the shadow of someone like Ethan Otis Allen looms large. As the writer of Hebrews asserts, "though he is dead, he still speaks" (Hebrews 11:4).

In Faith Healing: What I Have Witnessed of the Fulfillment of James 5:14–16, Allen has plenty to reveal about the audacious beauty of divine healing. Let us hear his words.

FAITH HEALING

WHAT I HAVE WITNESSED OF THE FULFILLMENT OF JAMES 5:14–16

ETHAN OTIS ALLEN

FULFILLING MY DUTY

It has been approximately thirty-five years[1] since my mind was first turned to the subject of divine healing. Dear brethren[2] in Christ, I felt it was my obligation to provide testimony about this doctrine. Through this book, I hope to give my confession a broader circulation in the vineyard of the Lord[3] than I could by my bodily presence.

Perhaps, in writing this, I will encourage weak or afflicted saints to approach the Savior with confidence—touching the hem of His garment, receiving healing virtue, and being made whole of their infirmity.

The Lord has accomplished great things, rescuing me from several diseases.[4] Still, I am not a unique object of Christ's healing power. In these last days, I have witnessed the demonstration of His power among many.

In the following, I will point out some of these cases along with my own.

I feel inadequate in this task. I have no reason for boasting. Only in the Lord do I find strength and confidence—knowing that He is my all and in all.

In these pages, I present some of my particular encounters as well as those of a few of my brethren and sisters. I pray that it will benefit some of the afflicted members of the Body of Christ.

MY INITIAL HEALING ENCOUNTER

In 1846, my mind first considered the subject of healing. I had been in poor health for several years because of a liver disorder, and at this time, the pain in my right side was nonstop.[5] There was a deep-seated soreness there. It was only with the sharpest pain that I could work.

One day in June, I got up, feeling like I was unable to labor. I had two brethren working for me, and at night, it was suggested that I should go to a schoolhouse a little ways away to have a time of prayer.[6] I had been thinking that day how Christ used to heal the sick, and I believed He could heal me if I could only exercise sufficient faith.

We went, and Brother Nathanael Pease opened the meeting. I accompanied him in prayer. Up to this moment, the pain in my body was like an obstacle. After praying a few words, the illness made me feel I was disconnected from the throne of grace. But I started to think: "Why don't you take your body along with you as you seek God?" I determined I would, and for the first time, felt free to tell God I was sick and needed help.

I laid my infirmity before God, grasping hold of the Savior as confidently as if He was personally present. I told Him about the throbbing in my side and how I believed He could restore me. I claimed the promise, and in a moment, was blessed in such a wonderful way.

I knew that the Lord heard my plea. The evidence of His hand was particularly clear. So, I started to praise the Lord, proclaiming, "I am healed! I am healed!"[7]

Satan was not far off, and he soon undertook to thwart the work. As I started home, a sharp pain started on my side. I still held on in faith, claiming I was healed —pain or no pain. I trudged on, but the aching continued, and the tempter said, "You now have more pain than ever." I proclaimed that I had the confirmation —pain or no pain. "Begone, Satan! Begone pain! It is done! I believe it!" All pain and soreness left me, and I was as happy as I could be.[8]

The next day, I worked with the greatest ease and the least inconvenience that I ever had in my life. It seemed like the angel of the Lord or an unseen power bore the burden of my work for me. I felt strong in the Lord and the power of His might. To God, be all the glory!

The next Sabbath, at a church meeting, I had nearly forgotten to testify to this healing when the pain in my side suddenly returned, more deathlike than ever.

However, as soon as I opened my mouth to give testimony of what I had experienced, I was free from all suffering. The Lord's approval of me was as clear as the

noonday sun. O praise the Lord for His goodness to this
unworthy piece of dust.[9]

FIGHTING SICKNESS AGAIN

One morning, a few months later, I was besieged with a
fever. My first thought was I am not going to surrender
to it. Needing to travel a dozen miles for business, I set
out,[10] but soon, my whole body was throbbing with
fever and pain.

After making it about eight miles, I was obliged to
come back home. I went back to bed, and my
companion[11] got things together to break up my fever. I
was thinking about the fact that the Lord already healed
me once, and when He walked the earth, He healed
many diseases.

I began to pray, but unbelieving thoughts arose:
"Your fever will soon intensify, and your pains will be so
severe that you will lose your reason. Then you will not
be able to exercise faith."

Although medicine was brought in to me, I refused
to give up faith in Christ. I dared not take the drugs,
even though I was urged to do so by my friend. I started
to pray again:

O Lord, thou hast healed me once. I refuse to doubt
you. Wilt thou not heal me now? My head aches, my
bones ache, and I am in confusion. O Lord, I do believe
thou can heal me now, as bad as I feel. I will arise in
the name of the Lord!

I rose to get out of bed but was so dizzy that I fell back. I started repeating the following:

> O Lord, I believe. I dare not give it up. I do believe thou can heal me, pain, or no pain. I shall trust thee, sink or swim, live or die. I arise in the name of the Lord.

Shortly after that, I got up again, announcing, "In thy name, O Lord!" I felt that I had truly laid hold of the Savior.

I felt emboldened and went downstairs. I was unsure about going outdoors—unbelief assaulted me. I either had to move forward or go back. But I dared not go the wrong way. I had risen in the name of the Lord, and I resolved that I would go out in His name.

I had barely stepped out the door when the result was clear.[12] The work was done. In a few minutes, my fever and pain were gone, and I was happy. What I felt inside and outside was as bright as the noonday sun.

I was beginning to be led by the Lord in a way that I did not formerly know. I praised Him then, and I am still doing it now. He has shown unbounded goodness to me.

I was residing at this time in East Windsor, Massachusetts. In the spring of 1848, I moved to Westfield to take charge of the town's poor and manage the town farm.[13] Here my companion and I spent eight years of cheerful toil.

ANOTHER BATTLE

In 1851, I was violently attacked with dysentery.[14] Experiencing extreme pain and fainting, I could not get up without help. I thought of Brother King Hastings, who lived in a neighboring town. I wanted him to come and pray with me. But since I wasn't confident he was home, I did not send for him.

My companion, feeling anxious, urged me to let her send for a doctor. I agreed, but in a few minutes, I regretted it. The physician came, and I took the medicine he offered. After a few distressful days, I mended. In weeks, I was up and about again.

Nevertheless, I was still in a dreadful state of darkness. I thought if I had only trusted the Lord and not sent for a doctor, God would have given the power to take His arm and be healed. I had to keep wrestling with the darkness.

I realized I would never be content with where I was until I prevailed in another trial of faith. I was almost overjoyed to have the trouble come. I had to reclaim my lost faith before I could ever be genuinely satisfied.[15]

A few months later, while conducting my annual report to the selectmen,[16] I was attacked with fever once more. The ill-effects increased throughout the day. Though advised to take medicine, I determined that I would not.

As soon as my guests had left, I sought the hand of the Savior—the only physician that I would ever need. They went home, and I retreated to my secret place. I was glad to be alone with the Lord. I confessed dissatisfaction with myself for not maintaining faith during my last sickness. I begged God to pardon me for my unbelief and talked to Him about my present ailment.

My mind wasn't clear, but I tried to exert faith amid the personal darkness. I prayed to the Lord to aid me. I already concluded that Lord forgave sins. But now I took hold of the biblical promises of healing.

I believed that I could be made whole if I would only consecrate myself to God.[17] I knew that I would proclaim the victory just as soon as the Lord made matters clear with His leadings.

I made an act of consecration and approached the Savior to be healed of my ailment. I soon found my faith taking hold with increasing strength. The fever started receding. I shouted, "O Lord, I believe thou hearest me and are helping me."

It was such a blessed time for me. Through this experience, I felt I had a commission not only to confess what God had done for me but also to take Christ for my physician.[18]

I have been healed of fever six times—each incident was unique. However, since the last affliction, Christ has been my constant helper—in colds, rheumatism, dysentery, and diphtheria.[19]

In the following book, I plan to omit much from my personal encounters. A detailed report of all my healings would take too much space to detail. I will, however, recount some of my experiences—along with testimonies from others that I have been honored to pray with.

THE HEALING OF POLLY AVERY

Among the town's poor in Westfield was a woman named Polly Avery. She had been a diligent and hardworking girl, but because of an ongoing bout of fits,[20] they sent her to the almshouse.[21]

Avery had one or two fits a day for over eight years, and her mind seemed to be destroyed. She could, for example, read the time while looking at a clock but had no recollection of it as soon as she looked away.

Avery was sick and was running down fast. She couldn't raise her head or hands and had limited awareness of what was going on around her.

The physician said she would not live. I informed her brother, who lived nearby, about this. He informed me he couldn't leave his shop. Besides, if he came to visit her, it would resolve nothing. He said that some other family members might go, but he could not.

After her brother spoke, a burden came over me. I remembered the biblical promise: "When my father and mother forsake me, the Lord will take me up" (Psalm 27:10). Although he was a brother, the principle was still relevant.

I went to my private place of prayer at home—feeling a burden of pleading that promise and giving glory to Jesus. I received evidence that God heard my prayer and believed He would appear and take up her cause.

I went into Polly's room and found her no better. I silently praised the Lord and exclaimed in my heart, "Glory be to thee, Lord! I still believe thou hast heard my prayer and that thou wilt yet take her up according to promise, although she has been given up to die."

I saw no change the rest of the day, and the next morning, she still wasn't any better.

Temptation came over me. I kept reflecting on Polly's condition in my mind and wouldn't let up. However, while I was at the breakfast table, she opened the door from the sickroom and stood in the doorway, wrapped in a sheet, exclaiming, "I want to get out of this dreadful place!"

My wife took Polly back to our room immediately. The woman was totally restored. I never heard of her having a single fit afterward. Polly's memory was restored, and she could go back to housework and other responsibilities. She was now capable of earning a living and attending the church she previously belonged to.

When Polly's family saw her, they were surprised. I told them the Lord accomplished a mighty work. To Him be the glory and praise.

THE HEALING OF THOMAS GROSS

Thomas Gross was a man of respectable parentage and a member of the Methodist church. Fifteen years earlier, his family sent him to the hospital for insanity. Gross did well for a while, but finally, the madness resurfaced.

His mind grew dull, and his health declined. Gross was reduced to a mere wreck of a man.

His brother-in-law approached me one day and informed me of his condition. He told me that Gross would probably only survive a few more weeks. When I saw him, it surprised me to see him looking like a skeleton. Observing his irregular heartbeat, I didn't think he had much time either.

Mr. Ely, one of the selectmen, urged me to take Gross to the town farm so his friends could visit and bring items for his comfort. I complied, though under no requirement to do so.[22]

They placed Gross in my care, even though he was not a pauper like others in the house. He was as helpless as a child—so feeble I carried him in my arms. His mind was starting to shut down, and he became an immense burden.

From the beginning, I was reluctant to take on his case because things looked so hopeless. I knew that I should pray for him, but I didn't know how I should pray—it would be improper to ask God to kill him.

I petitioned God to bring back his ability to reason and restore him so that he could go back home. As I prayed, the Spirit of faith aroused in me. It became clear that the Lord was more concerned about Gross' case than I was.

I renewed my earnest intercession until the burden let up and was satisfied that the Lord was working in this matter.

Afterward, I noticed that Gross' mind was starting to

return. He conversed with others and gained weight. Because of the work of the Lord, I was no longer burdened with this "child." Gross became a man once more.

What joy I encountered! I praised the Lord because I knew that it was His work. I didn't discuss these thoughts with anyone at the time, but I have done so since.

Brother Gross went home to his family and soon became a portly, good looking man. Within three months, he gained weight. Gross said that he made it back up to one hundred and sixty pounds, which I had no reason to question. He said, "Brother Allen, if I were not sent to your place, I would not still be alive."

"It is all the Lord's work." I replied, "It is truly His work, and the glory belongs to Him."

My eight years at the town farm of Westfield were accompanied by many of the blessings of God.

THE HEALING OF SISTER PAINE

In the spring of 1857, I moved to Oakfield, Wisconsin in Fond du Lac County. I located a farm that I purchased in partnership with Brother Charles Bush. We both went out there to do a little good and make our families comfortable.

In the spring of 1860, I went back out East to visit old friends. For a few weeks before my journey, my health was poor, though I could still labor. Finally, I visited Springfield for a few weeks. I attended an Advent meeting on the Sabbath before I returned,[23] which was about the middle of May.

I was not interested in the meeting until a brother, a stranger to me, requested prayer for his wife. He alluded to the brethren interceding with her the night before, saying that she had been under trial and temptation and had not received the benefit she hoped for. The husband requested the brethren to pray for her healing.

I was led by the Lord to ask if I could go home with him. He granted my request, and soon we were at his house.

His wife was praying and expecting someone to attack the underlying cause. As we talked, I was first led to tell a few of my experiences and discuss the exercise of faith. Believing and receiving, not receiving and believing.[24] She seemed to understand the subject and asked me to pray. We united in intercession, and the Lord encouraged our hearts, though we did not feel assured the work was done.[25]

After the next meeting, we had another season of prayer and seemed endowed with greater power. I visited the following day and prayed again. Our faith prevailed. The work was done. Sister Paine was healed, and we ascribed the glory to the Lord. Amen. Even so, let it ever be.

CONTINUING TO WALK IN FAITH

I returned to Wisconsin, but before reaching home, I became bilious,[26] my kidneys and liver were inflamed.

This happened so quickly after praying with the Paine family that I sensed that it was the adversary's work.[27]

I made it home exhausted. I dragged about a few days, getting worse until I determined it was time to make my own case a subject of prayer.

Nothing would persuade me to take medicine. I had trusted God and was convinced that He would not leave me subjected to disease. I believed I could go to God and be healed, and the work of the adversary would be thwarted.

I went to the Lord without fear, expecting to be healed. I began to pray, and this question arose: "Are you willing to confess, publicly, wherever God asks you to share?" I felt led to say, "yes," and I knew that the Lord would make the next actions understandable.

I prayed again, believing and receiving. I told my companion that I thought I was better and that the Lord was my helper. I worked some for two days, feeling much better. On Sunday morning, I thought my countenance looked as healthy as ever, that sallow and bilious look that I had disappeared.

Since there was no meeting in our district, I walked to another area to participate in a prayer meeting. It was a good one, and I was strongly impressed to talk about the subject of healing. I advocated for this truth with scripture and someone else's case, thinking I would reserve my testimony for our evening meeting back home.[28] So, after speaking, I sat down.

When evening came, I did not bring up my healing. Perhaps it was because it was merely my neighbors and family. But in this, I made a blunder. I wasn't thinking about the original leading from the Spirit. I was not aware that the enemy was dictating my confession.

The next morning my previous disorder returned. I asked, "Dear Lord, what does this mean?" The silence about my testimony came to mind immediately. It felt dreadful to realize I had been so careless.

I could say, from my heart, that it was not a willful act of neglect. I forgot the promise I made to God. It was almost as if I had never made it. And now the sickness returned.

I saw the biblical promises about my healing, clearly, but somehow could not grasp them. But even in this trouble, I wasn't willing to let up. I couldn't reject my faith by taking medicine. I confessed several times that I had been healed. I resolved that if I couldn't maintain the trust, I would die. How could I ever say that I had more faith in medicine than in Christ?

I laid down quickly with severe pain racking my body. I was as aware of my situation as anyone else. With a clear mind, I constantly prayed to the Lord to give me the power to take hold of His promises. But no power was given to me.

My wife and my friends began to be afraid that I might die. In two weeks, my heart rate was erratic. At this point, I was sure I could not exercise faith without some help.

My friends wanted me packed in a wet sheet.[29] I said that I had no faith in that practice. They urged me to do it for their sakes, and I reluctantly consented. But doing that shut off the light of the divine force.

I groped for the wall, but everything was dark. I could not grasp anything. My faith seemed weaker. I was encouraged to try the wet sheet again. I said, "I shall not, even if it results in my death." They wanted to get a physician, but I said that nothing but faith in the Lord Jesus would save me.

My wife said, "You cannot live long like this. You had better do something!"

I replied that I would call for Brother Charles Bush and Brother Thomas Patterson, in whom I had the highest confidence. If faith and prayer could not save me, I must die.

They asked these men to pray in secret, and then as soon as possible, pray with me in person. The next morning, they arrived. I was much weaker and in a clammy sweat, knowing my time was short unless we prevailed in prayer.

After I called for these brethren, my light returned. I had no trouble believing I was the Lord's child, whether I lived or died. But I had no power of faith in the gift of healing.[30]

Brother Bush united all of us in prayer. But he seemed unusually weak. I tried to pray a few words but was quite faint. I said within myself, "Show me, Lord, if this is my last sickness, and I will give up. Yet, I want to live a little longer to endure a little more trial."

Brother Bush then became remarkably burdened by the Spirit. I sensed that it was his responsibility to lay hands on me in the name of the Lord. I said, "Brother Bush, if you feel a leading to lay hands on me in the name of the Lord Jesus, don't hesitate."

He did, and I took hold of the promise: "They shall lay hands on the sick, and they shall recover" with earnestness. Yes, with a real grasp of faith. My faith was restored. I knew that I could hold on despite what was going on inside and out.

Glory be to the Lord Most High! He gave me the courage to fight the good fight of faith and obtain victory in His name. As hands were laid on me, my faith was as vigorous as ever.

Thomas shouted and seemed to have a power that everyone in the room felt.[31] I had to hold on, by faith, a half hour or more, entering into warfare with the enemy. [32] In all of this, my faith began to be restored, and with that, I was able to cling to the promise. I hung on with a defiant grasp in the face of the adversary.

The pains in my head, side, and kidneys did not let up until the battle was over. I claimed the promise: "They will lay hands on the sick, and they shall recover." The work of Christ was done, and I believed that I would recover—pain or no pain.

Then I shouted and praised the Lord, commanding Satan and the pain to "Begone!" Then I exclaimed, "I am being healed now!"

Faith increased, and the signs became so clear that I declared, "It is done! It is done! I am healed!" Glory to God in the Highest. I have the evidence! I again commanded Satan and the pain to be gone in the name of the Lord Jesus.

Every ache left me, and I was as happy as I could be in body and mind. The victory emerged after being completely shorn of faith for about three weeks. God, in His mercy, restored my faith through the laying on of hands by Brother Bush of Oakfield, Wisconsin, on July 8, 1861.

I still praise the Lord for this most remarkable deliverance from the most trying situation I ever experienced. By this, many of the brethren and sisters were convinced that the Lord could genuinely heal these days.[33]

THE HEALING OF ELIZABETH MAXON

The next case that I would like to discuss is that of Sister Elizabeth Maxon, widow of James Maxon, a Methodist preacher. Not long after my healing, I discovered that this depressed young woman had been sick for five weeks. The council of physicians didn't think they could help her. The consumption[34] seemed to be advancing quickly. She was flush, had an erratic pulse, and one lung was nearly consumed.

She wasted away for three more weeks and was so weak she was unable to sit up long enough to have her bed made. Much prayer was offered by the brethren at home and abroad, yet she continued to get worse until all hope of recovery was gone.

Brother Bush visited her, and she requested others

come and sing. Later, five of us came to meet with her. She asked Brother Thomas Patterson to pray. He did, and the other men united with him.

Then she called on each man, one at a time, to intercede. The spiritual agreement within the group was so strong we could have been called a five-fold cord. I was the least among these men.

Finally, she said, "Brother Allen, pray." I said, "Sister Maxon, I cannot pray. The Holy Ghost is already here. The prayers have been answered. Everything is ready. Have what you want."

Then she said, "Brother Bush, lay your hands on my lungs, and I will be healed." He was burdened for her breakthrough. Yet, feeling a little reluctant, he hesitated.

Maxon repeated her request, "Brother Bush, lay your hands on my lungs, and I will be healed."

Bush finally did so in the name of Jesus, and Maxon immediately exclaimed, "I am healed! I am healed! Praise the Lord!"

She called for her clothes and asked to get up and walk. Her family was not comfortable with this request. The last time she was up, things worsened, and they had to make her bed abruptly.

Yet, she praised God, celebrating the fact that she was healed! She insisted on getting up and walking around the room.

The glory resting on her was something all of us saw and felt.[35] There was no doubt that this wonderful work was done according to her faith. We advised her family and friends not to stand in the way of her worshipful response.

Brother Bush and all of us left the room, and Maxon got out of bed. When her family took hold of her shoulders, she was able to walk several times across the floor.

This was a mighty work of God through the prayer of faith and the laying on of hands in Jesus' name. To Him be all the glory! We had a most joyful time in rendering praise to the Lord.

The next morning the doctor found her at the breakfast table taking food instead of medicine. "What is going on?" he exclaimed. "It would not have surprised me if I had found you dead."

She told him, frankly, that the Lord had healed her. The doctor was even more surprised when he found that her pulse was normal. Thus, the fire in all her systems was extinguished through the laying on of hands by Brother Bush.

Without doubt, if the Lord had not made use of this healing gift, Sister Maxon and I would now have been asleep in Jesus, awaiting the morn of the resurrection.

For about a year or so afterward, this neighborhood became one of the sickliest places in the state. Every family had at least one case of fever—some two and three. One household had seven cases and two deaths.

THE HEALING OF FANNY PAINE

The next incident that I'd like to discuss concerns a woman who became mentally deranged by engaging in spiritualism.[36] Sister Fanny Paine was feeble and had been for some time. She had been a schoolteacher but had become too weak for work. She was often exhausted as she made it back to the boarding house she was staying at each night.

Some spiritualists, who were also lodging in the boarding house, tried to extend their delusion. They wouldn't let up until they made Fanny into a believer. These occultists failed for a time but slowly broke down her defenses.

Finally, the spiritualists persuaded Fanny to enter their circle and lay hands on the table. They brought her under their influence, and after that, she became demented. They could not undo what they had done, and Fanny was transported home—now a raving maniac.

It did not seem possible a woman could survive with so little nourishment and rest, but she went without it for several weeks. Fanny received prayer from a brother in Waupun, and it provided some help. Yet she was still partially bound and was concerned that she could not extricate herself from the darkness.

Fanny was carried to her sister's house a little way from my home. Her excitement[37] abated, but she was still in a gloomy state.

Fanny came to my house one morning with such a sick and sad countenance. It was the worst I had ever witnessed. She said she wanted out of this dreadful burden but was overwhelmed. She wanted me to invite some praying brethren to intercede for her. I did so.

That evening, we waited for Brother Bush. He had a hectic day. It had been rainy and chilly, and he felt too weary and out of sorts to do any good.

Bush finally appeared and took his seat. In a few minutes, he felt a leading from the Lord. Bush rose, crossed the room, and laid hands on Sister Paine's head. He announced, "O thou spirit of demons, I command thee in the name of the Lord Jesus to come out of Fanny. Arise, Fanny, in the name of the Lord Jesus."

She countered, "I will arise in the name of the Lord Jesus." She got up and walked out onto the floor. The evil spell that bound her was broken. The Satanic power was gone. There was such a visible shift in her countenance that no one doubted what happened. Afterward, Fanny was in an excellent state of mind.

We ascribed the praise and glory to the Lord for this mighty deliverance. We offered praise and thanks. Truly this occurrence transpired in a way that I did not anticipate.

Oh, I praise the Lord for His goodness to His children under all circumstances. Truly their deliverance is by His power, and in Him, do we ascribe the glory!

THE HEALING OF MARGARET TAYLOR

Sister Margaret Taylor, the wife of James Taylor, had a dangerous affliction after the death of her only son,

Willard. Over the weeks, she was providing constant care for her child and had no rest. Margaret broke down with a severe fever and had to remain in bed for five weeks. About the fourth week, I visited and found her terribly sick. I brought up the subject of healing to some of her friends. They did not seem to want me to pray. Yet, Sister Taylor's sister, Miss Patterson, confidentially said, "I wish you would get some of the brethren to pray for her. She grows worse every day. I don't think the doctor can cure her."

I felt apprehension and spoke to Brother Bush, assuming that he would feel the burden to labor under the Lord's direction. But he did not do anything. I did not have the courage to pray for her. So, I did not.

Things changed considerably one week later. I was visiting Brother Henry, a local preacher, who was likewise very sick. After being there a moment, I felt an unexpected unction from the Lord to go and see Sister Margaret Taylor. As this came over me, I let up on my prayers for Brother Henry. I knew that I had to shift my attention.

I dared not continue ministering in the Henry home —for I committed to responding to every leading from God. I told the Lord that I would go immediately. I altered my plans and started over to Brother Taylor's house.

When I went there, I found Sister Taylor being carried, in great distress, from one bed to another. Her family wondered if this could help her feel better. But the effort was in vain. Margaret only grew worse.

As they carried Sister Taylor back, she noticed me through the kitchen door and said, "Brother Allen, have you come to pray with me?"

I answered, "Yes, if you wish?"

"I do," she said.

I asked her brother, Thomas Patterson, to take hold of these matters with me. We knelt at her bedside. I had an unusual spirit of faith and prayer given to me—a power to take hold on to the arm of the Lord. I asked Him to stretch forth His hand to heal.[38]

Sister Taylor said, "Reach out with your hand." I wasn't sure what she was talking about. But her cry was so heartfelt that I knew that I had to keep interceding. All at once, she reached out her hand and grabbed hold of mine.

At that specific moment, I exclaimed, "It is done!" And as I made that declaration, she simultaneously proclaimed, "I am healed! Praise the Lord!"

Kneeling near me, Brother Patterson got excited. He started shouting, as he tended to do after receiving witness that the victory was obtained.

We had been on our knees a few minutes praying. Then I asked if Brother Thomas and I might keep praying for Sister Taylor for the rest of the night.[39] I felt impressed of the Lord that I must stay and battle against the enemy. Her mother permitted us to continue praying until morning.

This loving mother had been an excellent nurse. She made sure the erysipelas sore[40] on her daughter's foot was cleaned and adequately cared for. She placed a poultice[41] on it, of which I knew nothing about until morning.

About two hours after being healed, she awoke with distress in her stomach. I said, "Sister, look away from your pain and turn toward Jesus. He has healed you! Believe it."

"Yes," she said, "Praise the Lord. The pain is all gone."

I encouraged her to praise Jesus, and she soon fell back asleep.

Two hours afterward, the enemy made another assault. She was seized with severe pain in one arm that she shrieked in agony.[42] I could not get her attention quickly enough.

Brother Patterson and I knelt beside her but could not pray. I eventually rose and declared, "Oh, thou spirit of demons, in the name of Jesus Christ, I command thee to come out of Sister Margaret's arm."[43]

She affirmed, immediately, "There, it is gone. Praise the Lord!" I knew that the primary battle had been fought and won.

It was a happy time for Brother Thomas and me. He was alongside me in nearly every ministry effort. When I commanded sickness to leave in the name of Jesus, he agreed with me, saying, "Yes, go devil!"

I never labored with a brother who could get in there with me as effectively as Brother Thomas.[44] Neither of us was as strong in the Lord as others, but we could both pull in one direction at the same time.

In the morning, I suggested that we all offer thanks to God for Sister Taylor, who was truly healed. Oh, such a time we had, it was overwhelming. Sister Taylor's mother caught the Spirit and praised the Lord, saying, "I will trust my daughter in thy hands. I will not so much as put another poultice on her foot."

The mother was true to her word. All the inflammation came out of her body, and all was soon well.

The next morning, the doctor received a friendly dismissal from the family and another testimony of what God had done for his patient. Thus, the Lord accomplished remarkable things. To Him be the glory!

THE HEALING OF MINNIE MAXON

In the spring of 1861, Brother Bush and I sold our farm.[45] Things began to change for both of our families.

In the meantime, Sister Maxon's daughter was attacked with a severe fever. The mother, remembering what the Lord had previously done for her, turned to prayer but did not prevail.

Within weeks, the girl became so sick that friends and neighbors became alarmed. Though encouraged to do so, Sister Maxon felt she should not send for a doctor. She called for Brother Thomas Patterson and me to pray.

When we came, we found the girl with her eyes rolled up into her head. By natural appearances, it seemed foolhardy to think she could ever be healed. But we were not dismayed.

I felt assurance in the Lord and knew that He was stirring up the Spirit of faith and prayer in me. We knelt, and the whole gathering united with me in prayer. We took hold of the biblical promises, but Sister Maxon seemed to fall behind in her faith. I paused and urged her to believe along with me. She instantly broke out in prayer. All of us were unified, and the mother's faith brought things to a focal point. Soon we could all proclaim, "It is done! She is healed!" We thanked God and gave Him the glory.

As this mother arose, I never saw such a visible change in such a short time. Her countenance was natural and healthy, and her eyes bright.[46] I think the entire exercise took less than half an hour.

I was planning to be away on business overnight, but the Spirit revealed that a trial would soon follow.[47] When I found out that Brother Patterson was going away, I told Sister Maxon that she should not be troubled if the child appears to be sick again. If she would trust God, the trial would quickly end.

The next day at noon, the disease appeared to return. Sister Maxon, amid a deep trial, wept and prayed against the adversary. At first, it looked as though she might lose the battle. But Maxon pleaded, and the Lord answered. In Jesus' name, she triumphed, and the enemy retreated. Minnie was well again. Praise the Lord!

Towards evening, I called on the family and found the

girl looking so good that I exclaimed, "Truly, the Lord has healed. Praise His name!"

THE HEALING OF CHARLES BUSH

In January 1861, my family and I moved back to Westfield, Massachusetts. Brother Charles Bush and his wife were still in Wisconsin, living in the town of Waupun, five miles from our former residence.

In the winter of 1863, Brother Bush's family telegraphed a family member in Westfield, saying that Charles had a stroke and was suffering from paralysis. The doctors thought he would not live much longer.

It was a severe case. Bush couldn't move his toes or fingers. He could only see through one of his eyes. For three days, he was unable to speak. The left side of his body was entirely paralyzed.

I had worked with Brother Bush in business, praying for the sick, and in prayer meetings. I had a deep attachment to him. He was almost like a relative. The news of his calamity disturbed me. As I prayed, I felt sure I would soon hear that he was better.

In a few days, I heard that Brother Bush could see and move on his paralyzed side. In a few weeks, I found out he had recovered even more strength.

However, after that, Charles' health surprisingly grew worse, and it was requested that I visit him in Wisconsin. The doctors thought there were signs of another stroke coming at any moment.

I heard the news about Brother Bush on Saturday

and set out on Monday. I made all the railroad connections and finally reached Waupun, where Brother Bush's son was waiting at the depot.

I had a most joyful reunion with Brother Bush and family at his home. As I learned about his symptoms, I felt that my faith in God would prevail.

Before arriving in Wisconsin, I rededicated myself to God.[48] I was confident, knowing Brother Bush's faith that we would prevail if we came together. If needed, I would bring in more of the brethren that we used to labor alongside us in ministry.

It was between eight and nine o'clock at night when I arrived, so I began to rest, having traveled over a thousand miles without sleep.

I opened my heart to the Lord and prayed that He would show me in His word, a vision at night, or a leading through His teaching where I might go in the morning.[49] I wanted to get my Oakfield brethren to join us, for I had confidence in their faith.

In the night, my mind passed through a process that I did not understand, and in the morning, I had no specific leadings.

I knew something must be done and was pondering about what to do when Brother Bush's daughter rushed in, saying, "Mr. Allen, we want you to go upstairs quickly." She was afraid that her father was going into a convulsion.

When I reached the foot of the stairs, someone said, "Come quick!" Then, Sister Bush also called out to me. None of these anxious cries disturbed my faith.

I stepped up to Charles, who was lying on the lounge and said, "Brother Bush, I came to see you, and I will lay hands on you in the name of the Lord."

All at once, his countenance was changed from a sallow[50] to a moist, healthy-looking one. He exclaimed, "Why, Lucy, the most pleasing sensation has gone through my paralyzed side—clear down to the end of my toes."[51]

In a moment, Bush got up and started to walk. His wife, Lucy, blurted, "That beats all I ever saw! I did not believe in any such things, but now I have got to believe."

Brother Bush said, "You do not know what the Lord has done for me." He informed me he had not been able to put his left foot forward since the stroke. He had been crippled from that time until now. We walked the room together and praised the Lord, for we were truly blessed.

Soon Brother Bush ordered his horse and coach. We rode five miles to our old neighborhood, where we stayed for three days. The brethren were holding a protracted meeting.[52] It was a joyful time to be with my beloved Brother Bush and my old brethren. But best of all was a constant approval of the Lord. His blessing rested on us day and night.

Oh, in remembrance of those days. I still praise Jesus' name for His unbounded goodness to me. His loveliness was most gloriously unveiled in all His leadings and teachings.

Since then, I have been more and more assured that the Lord led me in a way I did not know. He empowered me to move in ways I had never done before. I never had a notion of laying on hands until I raised them in the prevailing name of Jesus.

I eventually came back home in the spring from Wisconsin and resettled in Springfield, Massachusetts.

ADDITIONAL HEALINGS IN THE PAINE FAMILY

In the next case, I have requested Sister Paine share it in her own words. Please keep in mind that this statement is merely one portion of her many healing encounters.

* * *

For a long time, I wanted to express my gratitude to God for His faithfulness and the fulfillment of His promises when I was severely afflicted. I share this for the encouragement of God's children who are traveling the same path. It is now nine years since God graciously appeared on my behalf to rebuke disease and answer the prayer of faith.

Brother Whitney was holding a series of meetings in Springfield, Massachusetts. Great enthusiasm arose. He was a man of faith and felt that people would benefit from his visit to this town. Before he came, I had suffered much and consulted many doctors, but similar to the "poor woman" in the Scriptures, I was no better. I grew worse.

Brother Whitney appealed to the Epistle of James,

and honestly, the result followed the pattern of the Word: "The prayer of faith shall save the sick." The blessing came. I went on my way rejoicing and would answer with the Psalmist "O that men would praise the Lord for His goodness and His wonderful works to the children of men" (Psalm 107:31).

But this Psalm also references other circumstances. Troubles arise, despite our precautions. Things occur that entangle us in troubles. Fortunately, the Bible affirms: "Then they cry unto the Lord in their troubles, and He saveth them out of their distress" (Psalm 107:13).

In the spring of 1866, I—Sister Paine—was brought low again. I appeared to be sinking into the arms of death. Medicine afforded no relief. The enemy seemed to gain the advantage. Still, I recalled how graciously the Lord had appeared for me and was encouraged by that precious promise: "None of them that trust in Him shall be desolate" (Psalm 34:22).

I requested some friends unite in prayer on my behalf, but the blessing did not come as it had before, and "hope deferred" made my heart sick. Nevertheless, when the desire came, it was a well-spring of life, for it did come (Proverbs 13:12). I started reflecting on Job 33:20–24, concentrating on the wisdom of the "interpreter."

On Sunday morning, I requested they ask the brethren at the church meeting to remember me in my time of affliction. When they presented my request, Brother Allen, who had come from the West, felt a compelling inclination to visit me. At the close of the meeting, he asked the privilege of doing so.

Allen, a total stranger, came and was like the interpreter from the Book of Job. He presented his experiences and talked about the Lord's way of dealing with people. While he prayed, faith sprang up in my heart.

From that day, I returned to my household duties. I had an increase in strength and vitality. My mind was peaceful, like a child resting on its mother's bosom. I was free from care as everything was cast on Jesus, who so mercifully cared for me. I wanted to praise Him for the past and trust Him for the future.

Not long afterward, my infant became so sick it was like he might die. It was a painful trial. At first, I gave him medicine, but I became convinced that I made a mistake. I remembered what God did for me and determined to place my child in the same hands.

Our thoughts ran wild as we watched our child suffer. The struggle brought back to mind our older child who died three years earlier from the same disease. The best medical aid couldn't save him.

The Word tells us that "Men ought always to pray and not faint" (Luke 18:1). We were inspired to more earnestly seek a manifestation of the Lord's healing power. Jesus did intervene, the disease was rebuffed, and our hearts were made glad.

And now, six years later, Jesus became our kind and faithful physician. He is the one we can depend on any hour of the day or night. Some imagine that a life of faith is one of laziness and indifference. It is, in fact, the very opposite. I urge one who dismisses it actually to try it for themselves.

Another thing is certain—those who embrace this way of life will find that self-denial is necessary. After all, nature's laws cannot be violated with impurity.[53] An individual may ignorantly bring disease on themselves and their children. When Jesus rebuked disease, He also said, "Sin no more, lest a worse thing come upon thee" (John 5:14). Such a decree places substantial weight on the conscience.

In February 1865, I became so sick that I could not sit up and could only speak a little. My companion was frightened and started seeking aid. My health was deteriorating fast.

Remembering what transpired in the past, I honestly could not lose faith in God's power or His readiness to help me. United prayer was offered up, and the refreshing presence of God came upon us. Although resting in the Lord, I still could not grab hold of the healing promise.

The disease continued to afflict me, and the next morning I was so fearful that I became slightly anxious. But the God who hears the ravens (Psalm 147:9) heard our cry and sent deliverance.

Brother Ethan Allen visited us. He pleaded my case before God as I rested with my companion. He laid my need before the Lord and grabbed hold of the scriptural promises.

In the meantime, Satan continued to attack my body, and I could not get myself free.

Upon a return visit, Brother Allen saw my anxiety and was led to lay hands on me, speaking peace in the name of Jesus. Very shortly, all within me was calm, peaceful, and trusting.

My companion spoke about the power that brought David out of the pit. It was an all-sufficient power. Suddenly an influence came upon me, penetrating every part of my being like an electric shock.[54] Then, an almost overwhelming sense of the goodness of God inspired me to shout, "Glory to God, the work is done!" I could join David in stating, "He hath brought me up out of the horrible pit and miry clay and established my goings and hath put a new song into my mouth, even praise to our God" (Psalm 40:2).

With steadfast assurance, I could step out in Jesus' name, leaning on Him for strength. Things rapidly increased, and I was again able to take charge of my family. It became apparent to all that it was "the Lord's doing and marvelous in our eyes" (Psalm 118:23).

Three months later, my faith was tested again by a similar attack. This time, I was brought so low as to feel that my breath was leaving my body. My companion proposed calling a doctor. I said, "Don't. If you do, you will lose me. No, no, live or die, I am the Lord's, and I will trust Him."

My companion expressed willingness to surrender me into the Lord's hands. The situation was dire. My faith was tested to the uttermost. But the Lord graciously appeared.

Upon my confession of faith in Jesus, during this trying hour, healing virtue came down on me with such power that I could not doubt. And though the enemy tried to keep me down once again, faith finally triumphed. God was glorified in the fulfillment of His promise, "The prayer of faith shall save the sick" (James 5:15).

I am thankful for the hope and confidence I have in the Lord amid the afflictions of this life. I can say with the psalmist, "God is our refuge and strength, a very present help in time of trouble" (Psalm 46:1), and "Blessed are all they that put their trust in Him" (Psalm 2:12).

I could present more of the Lord's gracious dealings with our family in rebuking disease, but enough has been said to prove it is the privilege of every child of God. All the Lord's precious promises are "Yes and amen in Christ Jesus" (1 Corinthians 2:20).

May God grant a great outpouring of His Spirit to His people. In these times of degeneration, may Christians walk in harmony with His Word. Let us live in such a way that the righteous and the wicked can be easily distinguished. People should know the difference between those that serve God and those who do not. This is the sincere prayer of the Lord's unworthy children.

Ann Paine

Springfield, Massachusetts
April 7th, 1866[55]

THE HEALING OF SAMUEL OTIS

The next case I will mention is the restoration of the child of Samuel Otis of Springfield, Massachusetts. The infant was taken sick at about seven months old. This disease was beyond the skills of the physicians. They didn't think that there was any hope for the child outside of faith and prayer. The family agreed to call for me.

So, early one spring morning, in 1865, Brother Otis drove out to my house and greeted me with the following question: "Brother Allen, are you full of faith and the Holy Ghost?"

I answered, "I was last night. I have not examined myself today, but I don't think the Lord has left me."[56] He then made known what he set out to do, and in a few minutes, we started for his house.

We discovered the child in considerable distress, rolling around on its head. The fever was no doubt impacting the brain. Brother Otis gave me the freedom to make any necessary arrangements.[57] So I requested one of his daughters to take the child. Then I had the mother kneel with us. I called on Brother Otis to pray. He started but was swallowed up in grief about his child. He halted.[58]

The Lord gave me unusual courage, and I received a burst of the spirit of prayer. When I released that utterance, it was as far as I could go by just prayer alone.

Without hesitation, I laid hands on the child in the name of Jesus. The child screamed,[59] and the mother rushed by its side. I was praising God and exclaiming, "Lay hands on the sick, and they shall recover" (Mark 16:18).

The child's eyes instantly brightened, and a lady sitting by said, "I don't think it will live. Its eyes are so changed." I urged them to believe that the child was better.[60] Brother Otis believed it, and in ten minutes, no one could doubt it.

Within fifteen minutes after hands were laid on the child, the infant nursed quite easily. This is something that the child had not been able to do for forty-eight hours. This put an end to the unbelief.

In the evening meeting, Brother Otis confessed what the Lord had done, and the sister who sat by during the prayers admitted that she saw the change—though she had no faith until she witnessed the healing.

God brought this to pass, and I believe we will heartily ascribe the praise to Him in grateful commemoration of His goodness.

MAKING A FAITH CONFESSION

I think I have written what is necessary about my healing experiences. Now, confessions should also come from others who have been blessed and are a means of blessing to others.[61]

How can Christians maintain a living faith in the gifts and callings of God without making a public confession? "For with the mouth confession is made unto salvation" (Romans 10:10).

During the last twenty years,[62] I have had the opportunity to confess many occasions in various places. Some wanted to hear what I had to say, but others thought my experiences were merely fanaticism.[63]

While out West, I once visited a quarterly Methodist love feast.[64] Being a guest, I knew that I shouldn't speak. The Holy Spirit seemed to circulate freely in the meeting, and I enjoyed it very much. But, all at once, I felt led to speak on the gift of healing and of what the Lord had done for me.

The meeting house was crowded, and three ministers were in the pulpit. I didn't know what I might be stirring up if I spoke. So, I just arose and poured out my heart to the congregation. I was genuinely worried that I might put a damper on the meeting. But I recognized the burden that the Lord placed on me, and I determined I would honor it. I would have to let the Lord take responsibility for any adverse reactions.

To my amazement, several also confessed their acceptance of the doctrine of healing. One of the advocates was the president of the meeting. This Methodist leader said that he had believed in healing for twenty years. He once disclosed some of his views, privately, to a brother in ministry but did not share his views openly. Due to this silence, the Methodist received little benefit from this faith.

Scripture plainly says, "Faith without works is dead" (James 2:14). This Methodist minister's testimony reflects the attitude of many these days. Although they know what is right, they are not speaking up for it. They are silent about the things of God.

Oh, ministers of Jesus Christ, why do you overlook this vital doctrine? Those who accept it, why don't you preach it and commit yourselves to it openly? Stand for faith so that the light may shine and that individuals will know where the sick can be sent to receive help!

Just because some backslide and are overzealous, we don't let faith in Christ for the forgiveness of sins be kept private. The same principle should be applied to our faith in Jesus' power to heal.

Don't let your light be hidden under a bushel. Stir up faith in the gift of healing. There is so much talk and so little accomplished.

The doctrine of holiness and healing are neglected by a majority of preachers and lay members of the church. Many seem to prefer escaping the criticism of the worldly.

But a backslidden church will never possess the Spirit of glory. Shall the believers "live by bread alone" or "by every word of God?" (Matt. 4:4). We must boldly affirm "the faith once delivered to the saints" (Jude 1:3).[65]

MINISTERS OF HEALING AND SIN-DESTROYING POWER

Dear brethren, dedicate yourself to the feeding of Christ's lambs. But also, be set apart to become nursing fathers and mothers in the church. Let Christ make you the ministers of His healing and His sin-destroying power. Christ healed and forgave sins at the same time. Why hold to the one and neglect the other? Why set one lamp on the stand and the other under a bushel?

Minister of Christ, your commission is the same as that of the apostles. If you accept the invitation and consecrate yourself to the Lord, you have a privilege to claim the same promises they had. If you're called of God, He will not forsake anything He pledged to perform.

Look at Christ's last commission to His apostles: "Go ye into all the world and preach the Gospel to every creature. And these signs shall follow them that believe. In my name, they shall cast out devils; they shall speak with new tongues; they shall take up serpents, and if they drink any deadly thing, it shall not hurt them. They shall lay hands on the sick, and they shall recover" (Mark 16:15-20 KJV).

Christ's promises provide guidance and help during moments of trouble. Believers shouldn't hunt up a deadly snake and frivolously handle them. However, when the venom cannot be evaded, there are promises for God's children. We live in a land of demons and sicknesses. Promises of deliverance, healing by prayer, and laying on hands are available—even in these times of apostasy.[66]

"Who hath believed our report? But though He had done so many miracles before them, yet they believed not on Him" (John 12:37). Perhaps unbelief is even more prominent these days than it was when Jesus walked the earth.

Many do not trust in God, but there are afflicted ones who will believe and receive the healing virtue. As scripture declares, "According to your faith, be it unto you" (Matt. 9:29). Christ's words were true eighteen hundred years ago, and they are true now. Try them, my afflicted brethren.

Christ, our Redeemer, says: "Is it easier to say your sins are forgiven or to say arise and walk? But that you may know that the Son of man has power on earth to forgive sins, I say unto you, arise, take up your bed and go into your house" (Mark 2:9–11).

This scripture indicates that it's just as easy to do one as the other. To forgive sins and heal is a work our Redeemer never refused while on earth. He is the same today. Believers should not limit Jesus' power by lack of trust. He repeatedly encouraged people to have faith in His Word, and He rebuked all unbelief.

I hope this little book, though written in simplicity and weakness, will be a blessing to many afflicted in body. This is the prayer of your unworthy brother in Christ.

–Ethan Otis Allen

"To forgive sins and heal is a work our precious Redeemer never refused to do when on earth. He is the same Savior today. Let us not limit His power by wicked unbelief."

—ETHAN OTIS ALLEN

PRELIMINARY THOUGHTS

HEALING PIONEER: REFLECTIONS ON THE LIFE AND MINISTRY OF ETHAN OTIS ALLEN

J.D. KING

Though underprivileged, Ethan Otis Allen (1813-1903) traveled extensively and interceded for myriads of people. Detailed records were not kept of his ministry, but healing testimonies were documented in handwritten letters and widely circulated journals.

Christians eagerly sought Allen out to pray for their diseased family members. To the delight of the afflicted, Allen would go anywhere and pray for anyone that God placed on his heart. He sincerely enjoyed caring for the needy.

Over the decades, Allen interacted with thousands and established lasting friendships with some of the most influential leaders of the era. The fruit of his life was not just the wondrous healings but also the nurturing relationships that he maintained. In many ways, Allen was a warrior with the heart of a father.

In the following section, we're going to encounter first-hand reports about the life and ministry of Ethan Otis Allen. Friends are going to share testimonies, personal reflections, providing an opportunity to learn a little more about this healing evangelist.

Read through these accounts and be reminded of how God works through the most unlikely people. The Lord uses frail, broken things to transform the world. There is hope for all of us.

HEALING PIONEER

REFLECTIONS ON THE LIFE AND MINISTRY OF ETHAN OTIS ALLEN

VARIOUS

WILLIAM TELFER MACARTHUR OF CALIFORNIA

I met Ethan O. Allen at the Old Orchard Convention over thirty years ago.[1] At that time, he was in his early eighties. He said that for more than fifty years, he did nothing but pray for the sick and the insane, or, as he expressed it, "Castin' out devils and healin' the sick." Small of stature and slight of build, he did not seem to carry more pounds than he did years.

When I inquired how Allen was directed into this particular line of service, he told me the story of his conversion and healing. He had tuberculosis and was disqualified for hard labor. So he was appointed superintendent of the poor farm. This rather crude institution was not only a home for the indigent but for the feeble-minded and harmless lunatics as well.

He did not remember what induced him to attend the Methodist class meeting being held in a country schoolhouse nearby. The night was dreary and wet, but the class leaders were earnest in their testimonies and prayers. At the close of the meeting, one of them said, "Brother Allen, don't you think it is time for you to seek religion?"

Allen was deeply impacted and responded to the invitation to come forward for prayer. How intelligently the subject was presented, he did not say. He simply recounted that he accepted Jesus as his savior and the unspeakable joy that filled his soul as a result. There was not only joy in the presence of the angels, but also in the presence of the class leaders who celebrated in the old-time Methodist style.[2]

After the demonstration subsided, he said, "Brethren, if you will pray for me, I believe this mighty power that has come upon me will heal my lung." A request like this was unheard of, and for a moment, the faith of the class leaders staggered.

At last one of them spoke up, and said, "Does it not say, 'They shall lay hands on the sick, and they shall recover?'" Then someone suggested that they try it. And to the astonishment of all but Ethan O. Allen, he was instantly and perfectly healed!

Returning to his duties as a poor master, he began to pray for the sick under his care. Considerable success attended his efforts; and while he knew that he was the subject of adverse criticism, the fact that the sick were

actually healed in answer to his prayers, encouraged him
to press on to greater achievements.

The passage of scripture referred to by the class
leader the night that Allen was healed was Mark 16:17-
18: "And these signs shall follow them that believe; in
my name shall they cast out devils; they shall speak with
new tongues; they shall take up serpents; and if they
drink any deadly thing, it shall not hurt them; they shall
lay hands on the sick, and they shall recover." He always
quoted this scripture as a basis of authority for all he
said and did.

In dealing with the epileptics and lunatics in the
institution, Allen learned to recognize a dual personality.
He saw that these unfortunate people were possessed
and controlled by extraneous intelligences, which could
be nothing other than the devils referred to in the words
of the "Old Commission," as Ethan called it.[3]

Little by little, he gained the courage to attack them
in the all-prevailing name of Jesus. Little by little, he
learned the power that name carried with it. To him, it
was an invincible weapon—not only a weapon of offense
but a shield of defense.

Allen once told me, "Young man, you look like
somebody the Lord could use in castin' out devils. I have
just one word of advice for you: Keep the name of Jesus
between you and the devil. He cannot come across that."
When Allen said that, he probably had in mind the
numerous instances in which he had been attacked by
the very diseases from which he had been instrumental
in delivering others.

Once, when I offered to help Ethan with his overcoat, he rejected it, explaining that while he had not been very strong previous to his seventieth year, since that time, he had been, "fust rate."

Allen told me of an experience he had in Philadelphia the previous fall, while he was "goin' out a-healin'" in the slush and snow. He got his feet wet and contracted typhoid fever. (No doubt the Schuylkill water he drank had its share in it.)[4]

He was unable to rise from his bed the next morning, and, not knowing anyone upon whom he could call to lay hands upon him for healing, he just laid hands upon himself. He lay there, unattended for thirty hours. Then the woman he rented the room from became alarmed and called the doctor. Allen said, "I jest shet up my eyes so they would not know I was awake."

The doctor told her that Allen had typhoid fever, and that, being an older man, he would not last long. He told her to keep him as comfortable as possible until the end came. When the doctor was gone, Ethan said he got up and took a bath, and found that his body was all covered with "yaller gum." "Then," he said, "I knowed that typhoid fever was the dirtiest thing that the devil could slap on to anybody. Then I put out some clean underwear and went out a-healin' again."

—William Telfer MacArthur (1861-1949) was a gifted orator and a pivotal leader in the Christian and Missionary Alliance after the death of A.B. Simpson.

EDGAR K. SELLEW OF MASSACHUSETTS

I was with Brother Allen more than fifty years ago in his prayer calls. He was settled in his convictions and would not go to any call until he had waited before the Lord for the Holy Spirit to witness to the call as being from God.[5]

He was in the habit of much fasting before the Lord. However, when the Lord spoke in his heart, nothing would deter him from the course that he thought was God's ordering.

He would not take a difficult case until he had fasted, and, in many cases, he insisted on fasting by the one who was sick.

He recognized Satan as the author of sickness and disease. He deliberately faced the evil one without fear. Whenever ministering, Allen proceeded first to "bind the strong man," or to expel the evil spirit.

At one time, Allen had on his cheekbone an open sore, which was diagnosed as cancer. As was his custom, he fasted and laid his own hands on it. He prayed and believed. Its growth was checked, but it persisted. Some time elapsed, and still, it was the same. I said, "Brother Allen, the cancer seems to persist in its work." He replied, "Oh, yes. I have not had time to attend to it." He had so much to do for others that he did not have time to fight the devil— fasting and praying until victory was manifested for him.

Time went on, and I met him at the Faith Home in Springfield, Massachusetts, and his face was fair and spotless. I said, "Oh, Brother Allen, praise the Lord!"

"Yes," he replied. "It dried up like a cot button held in place by a shank. One day I picked it off the floor, where it had dropped; it had a fiber coming out of the cheek attached to it like the shank of a button. Oh, I knowed it had to go." And we praised the Lord together.

A. B. Simpson[6] also spoke of Ethan O. Allen's testimony to him about the healing of the cancer on his face. He said that he had to keep taking life from God, and many times a day would lay his hands on the suffering place. He claims, at that moment, the very life of Christ was imparted to the diseased tissues and that the Lord was withering the malignant poison. On these occasions, he said that he was conscious of a current of life actually flowing into him from Heaven. After a few weeks of taking the Lord's life, the cancer withered away.[7]

My love for Allen, as an earnest Christian, began to grow about 1870. He came to my home to pray for my healing about 1880. Before this time, he was often away from home, being called to minister in distant places.

Brother Allen was also associated with Mrs. Sarah Mix,[8] a negro woman, in praying for the sick. Among other things, he was a visitor at Germantown, Pennsylvania, at Mrs. Sarah G. Beck's Kemuel House[9] and other institutions. He also met with English visitors, notably Michael and Elizabeth Baxter.[10]

Allen was very modest in manner, never pushing his views forward. But he was always ready to give a reason for the hope set within him. He was more simple, sane, and scriptural on the subject of healing than any other person I ever met.

There was a little Faith Home in Springfield, Massachusetts that he always supported, and he was conversant with a number of leaders in the faith line of teaching and laying on of hands for healing.

He was unique. He used his own methods and phrases. In ministering to the sick, I have no recollection of him ever praying until he first cast out the evil spirits. He believed that demons caused all diseases. When he prayed for me, his first words were, "Devil, get out of them legs!" He then laid on hands, and my varicose veins were free. There was never any more trouble. This was his custom: "First, bind the strong man."

Brother Allen and I journeyed to New York, attending the Alliance meetings where Isaac Hess was before he went to China.[11] A.B. Simpson paid Brother Allen great deference as the "Father of divine healing," and others in the meeting joined in showing him honor.

While in New York, Brother Allen met Mary Shoemaker and enlisted her help for starting the Springfield Faith Home. Miss Shoemaker came to Springfield and built "Shiloh Chapel," and put Rosa and Orpha in charge. All are now dead, and I know of no one who could give any more information.

Brother Allen's life was so simple, so sweet. He appeared to be commonplace to commonplace people. Only those who walked in the glory saw the glory which was upon Brother Allen.

—Edgar K. Sellew (1840-1915) of Springfield,
Massachusetts, was a lay evangelist and personal
friend of Ethan Otis Allen.

SARAH M. C. MUSGROVE, OF TROY, NEW YORK

My acquaintance with Ethan O. Allen began in a Home
for Incurables in Brooklyn, New York, on January 28,
1882, at 6 P.M. During these forty-two years, I have had
reason to praise the Lord for that first hour of
acquaintance with this man of God. For through him, a
humble, yielded instrument in God's hands, the Lord,
on my behalf, worked wondrously.

I had been sick nearly four and a half years—a
terrible sufferer. I had many of the best physicians. Their
verdict was that my entire body was so completely worn
out that recovery was impossible.

I had been taken to the Home for Incurables early in
the summer of 1881, with a letter to the matron saying,
"She may live until the leaves fall." Not one of my
friends expected I would ever leave that home alive.
Still, the Lord gave me the assurance that I should again
engage in Christian work.

God laid my case upon the hearts of two Christian
women in New London who were acquainted with
Ethan O. Allen's fruitful ministry on behalf of the sick.
They wrote to me, asking if they might send him to pray
for my healing. I asked the Lord if this was His will,

reveal to the caretaker of the home. Upon reading the letter, she said, "I believe this is God's will."

Word was sent to Ethan O. Allen, asking him to come. He knew the voice of God, and, as was always his custom, Allen inquired of the Lord what he should do. The Lord's answer was, "Go. I will raise her up for my glory." So, obediently, he took the journey from Springfield, Massachusetts, to Brooklyn, New York.

Arriving at the Home about supper time, he was asked to eat before praying with me. The reply was characteristic of this humble, obedient servant of the Lord: "No. The Lord has important work for me in this Home. I shall neither eat nor drink until it is accomplished."

Then, coming at once to me, very quietly, he asked me about my Christian experience. He offered a simple prayer, like a little child to its father, asking that He would verify His own Word.

Turning to me, he asked, "Do you believe that the Lord is able to heal you?"

"Yes."

"That He is willing to?"

"Yes."

"That He wants to do it now?"

"Yes."

Then repeating the words, "They that believe shall lay hands on the sick, and they shall recover" (Mark 16:18), he laid his hands on me in the name of Jesus, and told the Lord that he believed, on the authority of His Word, that I was healed. I also believed it.

Together, we praised the Lord for healing me. New life surged through my entire being. The forty-two years since that hour have proved the healing permanent.

Brother Allen's fast was not over. He still refused food on the ground that the Lord had showed him that there were other cases in that Home, and also outside of the home for whom God would use him. As long as this special session of ministry lasted, his fast continued. It was remarkable that when the fast ended, he seemed as fresh as at the beginning.

The Spirit bestowed upon Ethan Allen, in a marked degree, the gift of casting out demons. I might relate one case that occurred in the Home before he left.

When he was about to labor on behalf of a very friendly young woman, Allen asserted that she had a case of demon possession. Some of the inmates[12] present were angry that he should make such a statement, but he repeated it. Allen obtained her permission to minister along these lines.

As soon as he began to command the evil, tormenting spirits to depart, she became violent, even using physical force against him. The onlookers, at the same time, were criticizing him. But he was unmoved—resolutely continuing to command for the evil spirits to come out of her.

At last, she fell back on the bed as though dead, and some of the people excitedly cried out, "He has killed her! She is dead!" Very soon, she aroused and was praising the Lord, saying, "I am healed."

If Ethan O. Allen commenced a conflict against

demons, however severe the resistance, he would not give up the battle—in the name of Jesus—until they were routed and there was a decided victory.

At the beginning of my ministry in the Four-Fold Gospel in Troy, New York, Allen and I ministered together in some remarkable cases of healing.

To him, could surely be applied the following verses from the Word of God:

"Not by might, nor by power, but by my Spirit saith the Lord of hosts" (Zech. 4:6.).

"God hath chosen the foolish things of the world to confound the wise: and God hath chosen the weak things of the world to confound the things which are mighty . . . That no flesh should glory in His presence." (I Cor. 1:27, 29.)

—Sarah M. C. Musgrove (1839-1933) was healed under Allen's ministry and later ran the Fourfold Gospel Mission, a healing home in Troy, New York.

CARRIE JUDD MONTGOMERY OF BEULAH HEIGHTS, CALIFORNIA

"God hath chosen the foolish things of the world to confound the wise: and God hath chosen the weak things of the world to confound the things which are mighty" That no flesh should glory in His presence" (1 Corinthians 1:27, 29).

Now, regarding Ethan O. Allen, I suppose you mean the Mr. Allen who prayed for Mrs. Sarah Ann Mix when she was healed of tuberculosis many years ago. He used to take a great interest in me and called himself my "grandfather" because he prayed for Mrs. Mix's healing, and afterward she prayed for mine.[13]

Brother Allen surely was a dear, quaint, older man. Later in life, he spent some time in California and was with us at the Home of Peace[14]. We became very well acquainted. His piety and faith were marvelous.

Mr. Montgomery and I admired Allen very much in the Lord. He had an authority of faith to make the devil give up his hold, which was most inspiring.

I suppose that you have heard Allen tell the story about his pig. It was truly a wonderful story. He was praying with a girl who was demon-possessed and trying to cast the devil out. The demon was somewhat slow in obeying Brother Allen's command to depart. So, he finally said to the devil, "I tell you what I will do. I will let you go into my pig at home." The young woman was then delivered, as the demon gave up his hold.

Meanwhile, Brother Allen's wife Kekiah was at home and knew nothing about this occurrence. Only she noticed that something terrible had come over the pig. It apparently became insane and raced back and forth in the pen in a frightful way.

When Ethan finally made it home, she said, "Oh? Ethan, Ethan, I don't know what is the matter with our pig!" She described its unusual actions to her husband.

He said, "Well, I know what the matter is. I

permitted that demon to go into our pig, but I will not permit him to stay there."

So, Ethan proceeded to cast the devil out, and the pig was instantly delivered.

In one sense, this story is rather amusing. Yet, in another sense, it is full of teaching. Through it, people can realize the reality of demonic possession—whether in people or pigs.

It has been such a long time since Brother Allen was with us that I forget many details about his ministry. Some other stories I might have remembered if I had been asked for a testimony about him at an earlier date. Mr. Montgomery and I certainly felt it a great privilege to be acquainted with Brother Ethan Allen.

—Carrie Judd Montgomery (1858-1946) was healed of tuberculosis of the spine in 1877 and was an important figure in the Faith Cure Movement. She later joined the burgeoning Pentecostals and opened the Home of Peace in Oakland, California.

ANNA CASSEL REIFF OF CHICAGO

The Son of God is still transforming men of low degree into mighty warriors of faith. He delights in taking the weak things to confound the mighty, the foolish things to bewilder the wise.

God found Ethan Allen in the days when the doctrine of divine healing was in its infancy. With childlike simplicity, the poor master accepted this gift, using the words and methods employed by the Lord Jesus Christ when on earth.

To Allen, the devil was very real. He had many fierce conflicts with the unseen forces, but he was fearless, having complete confidence in the all-powerful name of Jesus.

A minister once wrote Ethan Allen to pray for a sick woman and received the following reply on a postcard: "All hail! I offered the words of castin' out as they were given to me by the Holy Ghost by the space of half an hour, and I feel sure the devil has gone out of the woman."[15]

The woman herself had been a teacher of divine healing and had seen many people healed in answer to her prayers. In the natural, she would have resented his "words of castin' out," but she was sick unto death and could get no help from God.

She finally called in several doctors, and they pronounced her case as hopeless. They were unable to agree in their diagnosis, but all admitted that she was beyond their help.

For some time, the woman remained in this helpless condition, and then the minister lost sight of her, having moved to a distant city. He often wondered about "Father" Allen's words of castin' out and whether, in this case, they had failed.

Five years later, he held a service in that same city, and a portly woman came and shook hands with him whose name he could not recall. He learned that it was the same woman whom he left in a dying condition.

"Tell me about it," he said. "There is nothing to tell,' she replied. All I know is that I awakened one morning to find myself in perfect health."

She had no faith, and apparently, no one else had faith for her, but God couldn't deny His servant, Ethan O. Allen, who had such childlike faith in Him.

—Anna Cassel Reiff (1869-1960) was John Alexander Dowie's general secretary and installed as a deaconess at his Catholic Apostolic Church. In 1911, she became the managing editor of the *Latter Rain Evangel*, a Pentecostal periodical published out of Chicago.

DEATH OF PIONEER HEALER BY PRAYER

ETHAN OTIS ALLEN (1813-1903)

E than O. Allen, better known as "Father Allen,"
a former resident of this city, died in Los
Angeles, California, on January 24, 1903.

Mr. Allen was a descendant of Ethan Allen of
Continental Army fame[1] and was born on the Allen
homestead on Allen Road, where he lived eighty-five
years. About five years ago, he moved to Los Angeles,
where he remained until his death.

Mr. Allen, although a quiet and unobtrusive man,
was widely known in religious circles. As a man of faith,
his name was familiar in all Christian lands to those of
his faith.[2]

He began his life work of praying with the sick for
their recovery over sixty years ago, basing his faith on
the belief that Christ's atonement covered the diseases
of the body as well as the sins of the soul.[3]

Mr. Allen was the first worker on this line in America

but was contemporaneous with Dorothea Trudel, who began her labors in Switzerland about the same time.[4]

Mr. Allen was a man of positive convictions, and of uncompromising integrity. He was generous to those in need, always genial. No apparent illness or suffering preceded his death. A wide circle of friends will miss him. He leaves no family, his only son having died in Los Angeles a few months ago.

—Editor, "Death of Pioneer Healer by Prayer," *Springfield Republican,* Springfield, Massachusetts (February 1903).

NOTES

INTRODUCTION

1. See Nancy Hardesty, *Faith Cure: Divine Healing in the Holiness and Pentecostal Movements* (Peabody, Massachusetts: Hendrickson, 2003). James Robinson, *Divine Healing: The Formative Years: 1830–1880: Theological Roots in the Transatlantic World* (Eugene: Pickwick, 2011). J. D. King, Regeneration: A Complete History of Healing in the Christian Church, vol. 1 (Lees Summit, Missouri: Christos, 2017).

FORGOTTEN FATHER

1. The Faith Cure Movement was a transatlantic healing revival that intersected with the Pietist and Wesleyan-Holiness traditions. It included such luminaries as Johann Christoph Blumhardt in Germany, Dorothea Trudel in Switzerland, Charles Cullis in Boston, and A.B. Simpson in New York. The Faith Cure Movement began in Europe in the late 1840s but didn't gain prominence in America until the 1880s.
2. The Pentecostal Movement first sparked in Topeka, Kansas in 1901, but later exploded in Los Angeles, California in 1906. In addition to speaking in unknown tongues, the participants in this burgeoning revival also prayed for the sick.
3. A. B. Simpson quoted in William T. MacArthur, "Ethan O. Allen" (Philadelphia: Office of Publication of the Parlor Evangelist, undated), 14. The Christian and Missionary Alliance was an influential revivalistic denomination in the late nineteenth century. Many of the leaders of the American Faith-Cure Movement were associated with this fellowship. See Kimberly Ervin Alexander, *Pentecostal Healing: Models in Theology and Practice* (Leiderdorp, Netherlands: Deo Publishing, 2006). Also, Paul G.

Chappell, "The Divine Healing Movement in America," Ph.D., diss., Drew University, 1983.

4. Poorhouses or poor farms were modest, government-run facilities erected to provide housing and support for the intransient and needy.

5. James Robinson, *Divine Healing: The Formative Years: 1830–1880: Theological Roots in the Transatlantic World* (Eugene: Pickwick, 2011), 127.

6. James Robinson writes, "The Methodist Episcopal Church (MEC) began to lose its countercultural reputation and became increasingly bourgeois in its ways from the 1820s." James Robinson, *Divine Healing: The Formative Years: 1830–1880: Theological Roots in the Transatlantic World* (Eugene: Pickwick, 2011), 124.

7. Ethan O. Allen quoted in William T. MacArthur, "Ethan O. Allen" (Philadelphia: The Parlor Evangelist, undated), 1.

8. For more on the healing experiences of Wesley and his Methodist associates, see Robert Webster, *Methodism and the Miraculous: John Wesley's Idea of the Supernatural and the Identification of Methodists in the Eighteenth Century.* Lexington, Kentucky: Emeth Press, 2013. Daniel R. Jennings. *The Supernatural Occurrences of John Wesley.* Oklahoma City: Sean Multimedia, 2005, 2012. Jeffrey R. Hiatt. "John Wesley and Healing: Developing Wesleyan Missiology." *The Asbury Theological Journal* 59:1–2 (Spring, Fall 2004): 89–109.

9. Paul G. Chappell, "The Divine Healing Movement in America," Ph.D., diss., Drew University, 1983, 54.

10. Orin Peer Allen, *The Allen Memorial: Descendants of Samuel Allen of Windsor, Connecticut, 1640–1907* (Palmer, Massachusetts: 1907), 165.

11. William T. MacArthur, "Ethan O. Allen" (Philadelphia: The Parlor Evangelist, undated), 3.

12. Paul G. Chappell, "The Divine Healing Movement in America," Ph.D., diss., Drew University, 1983, 92.

13. Ibid., 90–91.

14. In subsequent years, Allen was concerned that the Methodists "downplayed the distinctive doctrine of scriptural holiness as well as restraining the ministry of divine healing." James Robinson, *Divine Healing: The Formative Years: 1830–1880:*

Theological Roots in the Transatlantic World (Eugene: Pickwick, 2011), 129.

15. Allen did informally work alongside a number of people over the years. One of his earlier partners was a man named Charles Bush, who understood the realities of healing and instructed Allen. But he had no official affiliation with a ministerial association.

16. William T. MacArthur, "Ethan O. Allen" (Philadelphia: *The Parlor Evangelist*, undated), 3.

17. Allen combined demonic deliverance and spiritual warfare with a robust application of the gifts of the Spirit (1 Cor. 12:8-12). He conveyed a Charismatic spirituality a century before it became vogue in the United States.

18. See Dieter Ising, *Johann Christoph Blumhardt, Life and Work: A New Biography*, trans. Monty Ledford (Eugene, Oregon: Cascade Books, 2009). Friedrich Zundel, *Pastor Johann Christoph Blumhardt: An Account of His Life*, eds. Christian T. Collins Winn and Charles E. Moore (Eugene, Oregon: Cascade Books, 2010).

19. See Charles Cullis, *Dorothea Trudel; or, The prayer of faith, showing the remarkable manner in which large numbers of sick persons were healed in answer to special prayer* (Boston: Willard Tract Repository, 1879). There is no modern account of her life.

20. Ethan Allen had no direct knowledge of Blumhardt or Trudel in the 1840s and 50s. He simply applied what he was learning through study and practical experience. See James Robinson, *Divine Healing: The Formative Years: 1830–1880: Theological Roots in the Transatlantic World* (Eugene, Oregon: Pickwick, 2011). Also J. D. King, *Regeneration: A Complete History of Healing in the Christian Church*, vol. 1 (Lees Summit, Missouri: Christos, 2017).

21. The Bible uses the word "flesh" (Greek: *sarx*) uniquely. Rather than referring to a natural human body, it means the human condition in its fallenness. Allen defined his early healing experience as a work of "sanctification" and believed if individuals were purified from sin, they would also be healed. These notions are rooted in early Methodist and Wesleyan ideals.

22. Anna C. Reiff, "Miracles Wrought Through Prayer and Fasting: The Story of a Man who Walked with God," *Latter Rain Evangel* 22:8 (May 1930), 6.

23. Ibid., 7.

24. Ibid.

25. Paul G. Chappell, "The Divine Healing Movement in America," Ph.D., diss., Drew University, 1983, 99.

26. Ibid, 92.

27. Ethan O. Allen, "Satan Under Your Feet," (Undated).

28. Paul G. Chappell, "The Divine Healing Movement in America," Ph.D., diss., Drew University, 1983, 100.

29. It is interesting, but in contrast with later Pentecostals, Allen "laid less stress on the sufferer's faith than on his own gift of faith and inward assurance as to the outcome of his intercessory prayer." James Robinson, *Divine Healing: The Formative Years: 1830–1880: Theological Roots in the Transatlantic World* (Eugene: Pickwick, 2011), 128.

30. This passage became the central text for his ministry.

31. See Ethan O. Allen, "Satan Under Your Feet," (Undated).

32. William T. MacArthur, "Ethan O. Allen" (Philadelphia: The Parlor Evangelist, undated), 7.

33. James Robinson, *Divine Healing: The Formative Years: 1830–1880: Theological Roots in the Transatlantic World* (Eugene: Pickwick, 2011), 128.

34. Edgar Sellew quoted in William T. MacArthur, "Ethan O. Allen" (Philadelphia: The Parlor Evangelist, undated), 12-13.

35. William T. MacArthur, "Ethan O. Allen" (Philadelphia: The Parlor Evangelist, undated), 11.

36. Ibid., 7.

37. Paul G. Chappell, "The Divine Healing Movement in America," Ph.D., diss., Drew University, 1983, 100-103.

38. William T. MacArthur, "Ethan O. Allen" (Philadelphia: The Parlor Evangelist, undated), 7.

39. *Galveston Daily News* 43:165 (Sunday, October 5, 1884).

40. Paul G. Chappell, "The Divine Healing Movement in America," Ph.D., diss., Drew University, 1983, 101.

41. Ethan Allen quoted in Jonathan Richard Baer, "Perfectly Empowered Bodies: Divine Healing in Modernizing America," Ph.D. diss., Yale University, 2002, 41.

42. Sarah M. C. Musgrove quoted in William T. MacArthur, "Ethan O. Allen" (Philadelphia: The Parlor Evangelist, undated), 15-16.

43. See Editor, "A Long and Useful Life," *The Alliance Weekly* 69:3 (January 20, 1934), 39, 46.

44. James Robinson, *Divine Healing: The Formative Years: 1830–1880: Theological Roots in the Transatlantic World* (Eugene: Pickwick, 2011), 127.

45. Seth C. and Hulda A. Rees, "Testimony to Healing," *The Christian and Missionary Alliance* XVIII: 20 (Friday, May 14, 1897), 466. Seth Cook Rees was a boisterous preacher and a leading figure in the "holiness movement." He helped found the International Holiness Union and Prayer League, and later the Pilgrim Holiness Church, a forerunner of the Wesleyan Church.

46. Anna C. Reiff, "Miracles Wrought Through Prayer and Fasting: The Story of a Man who Walked with God," *Latter Rain Evangel* 22:8 (May 1930), 6.

47. Testimony from an unnamed man from Groton, Connecticut in W. J. Starr, "Touching the Hem of His Garment," *Triumphs of Faith* 2:3 (March 1882), 41.

48. The healing stories included in *Faith Healing: What I Have Witnessed of the Fulfillment of James 5:14–16* are not overly elaborated. Allen often shares them in a brief, matter-of-fact tone. Most of this book appears to have been written in the late 1860s, so it does not include any of his later stories.

49. James Robinson, *Divine Healing: The Formative Years: 1830–1880: Theological Roots in the Transatlantic World* (Eugene: Pickwick, 2011), 129.

50. Ethan Allen, "Satan Under Your Feet" (Undated).

51. Paul G. Chappell, "The Divine Healing Movement in America," Ph.D., diss., Drew University, 1983, 92.

52. Ibid.

53. Ibid., 93.

54. Sarah Ann Mix, *Faith Cures, and Answer to Prayer: The Life and Work of the First African American Healing Evangelist*, ed. Rosemary D. Gooden (Syracuse, New York: Syracuse University Press, 2001), 210.

55. "Miraculous Cures in Connecticut," *The Buffalo Daily Courier*, February 20, 1879.

56. See Mrs. Edward Mix, *The Life of Mrs. Edward Mix* (Torrington, Connecticut: Press of Register Printing Co, 1884).

57. Paul G. Chappell, "The Divine Healing Movement in America," Ph.D., diss., Drew University, 1983, 93. Unlike many during this

era, Allen was neither sexist nor racist. He welcomed females and African-Americans to serve alongside him in ministry.

58. Terri Taylor found, between 1880 and 1915, sixty-five healing homes in North America. Each was pivotal to advancing the cause of Christ-centered rejuvenation. Terri Taylor, "Faith-Cure and Healing Homes." *http://www.healingandrevival.com/Faith%20Homes.htm* (accessed May 2, 2016).

59. Paul G. Chappell, "The Divine Healing Movement in America," Ph.D., diss., Drew University, 1983, 92-93.

60. Ibid., 103.

61. James Robinson, *Divine Healing: The Formative Years: 1830–1880: Theological Roots in the Transatlantic World* (Eugene: Pickwick, 2011), 126.

62. Ibid.

63. Paul G. Chappell, "The Divine Healing Movement in America," Ph.D., diss., Drew University, 1983, 103.

64. Ibid. Cullis, a homeopathic physician, was a graduate of Vermont College. Simpson was also well-educated and eloquent.

65. Ibid.

66. While this book was released in 1881, it contains material that was written earlier. The book was probably composed around 1870.

67. Paul G. Chappell, "The Divine Healing Movement in America," Ph.D., diss., Drew University, 1983, 127. Otto Stockmayer (1838-1917) of Germany wrote *Sickness and the Gospel* (1879). This work, rooting the doctrine of healing in the atonement, was pivotal for transatlantic Faith Cure teaching. A. B. Simpson (1843-1919) of the Christian and Missionary Alliance wrote, *The Gospel of Healing* (1885), another influential work on spiritual cures. A. J. Gordon (1836-1895), a prominent Baptist pastor and educator, wrote *The Ministry of Healing* (1882), arguably the definitive work on praying for the sick in the late nineteenth century.

68. Edgar Sellew, "Ethan Allen," *Christian and Missionary Alliance Weekly* (May 23, 1903), 289.

69. Anna C. Reiff, "Miracles Wrought Through Prayer and Fasting: The Story of a Man who Walked with God," *Latter Rain Evangel* 22:8 (May 1930), 8.

70. Edgar Sellew, "Ethan Allen," *Christian and Missionary Alliance Weekly* (May 23, 1903), 289.

71. Anna C. Reiff, "Miracles Wrought Through Prayer and Fasting: The Story of a Man who Walked with God," *Latter Rain Evangel* 22:8 (May 1930), 8.

72. William T. MacArthur, *Ethan Allen* (Philadelphia: Office of Publication of the Parlor Evangelist, undated). 2. Edgar Sellew, Allen's dear friend, said, "He fell asleep . . . There was no disease about him, only a giving out of the entire system." Edgar Sellew, "Ethan Allen," *Christian and Missionary Alliance Weekly* (May 23, 1903), 289.

73. Edgar Sellew, "Ethan Allen," *Christian and Missionary Alliance Weekly* (May 23, 1903), 289.

74. William T. MacArthur, *Ethan Allen* (Philadelphia: Office of Publication of the Parlor Evangelist, undated). 3.

75. James Robinson, *Divine Healing: The Formative Years: 1830–1880: Theological Roots in the Transatlantic World* (Eugene: Pickwick, 2011), 129.

PRELIMINARY THOUGHTS

1. The American Faith Cure Movement was a divine healing revival primarily among Holiness and Deeper life Christians in the last two decades of the nineteenth century.

2. The radical faith healing position emerged during the American leg of the Faith Cure Movement. Those who held this view—John Alexander Dowie (1847-1907), John G. Lake (1870-1935), and several early Pentecostals—believed doctors and medicine were the works of the devil. They declared healing was in the atonement and guaranteed to all who had faith. Most of the radicals believed that all diseases were demonically rooted.

3. William T. MacArthur, Ethan Allen, (Philadelphia: Office of Publication of the Parlor Evangelist, undated). 3.

FAITH HEALING

1. Allen was first healed in 1846, about thirty-five years prior to the publication of this book. Although portions were written around 1881, much of the book refers to events and experiences from the 1860s. It is likely that this book was started in the 1860s and then completed much later.

2. Allen uses the term "brethren" throughout this book as a way of describing devout Christian men.

3. The term "Vineyard of Lord" is Allen's way of describing broader, trans-denominational Protestantism.

4. In the first part of this book, Allen highlights his own struggle with disease. His goal was not to write a detailed biographical account, but to help his audience understand faith and Kingdom realities. Allen understood the reality of divine healing, not just because he prayed for others. He knew it because he wrestled with it personally throughout his life. The following paragraphs are meant to be instructive, not descriptive.

5. Allen apparently had a number of illnesses over the years. Those that knew him the longest referenced his early struggles with tuberculosis. This sickness seemingly affected several parts of his body including his liver.

6. This was an old-fashioned Methodist class meeting.

7. Allen's particulars are slightly different from some of the other accounts of his life. He, for example, minimizes the role of the Methodist evangelists that he was engaging with in the schoolhouse. Allen focuses here on guiding readers through his journey of growing in spiritual warfare.

8. Throughout this book, Allen focuses on wrestling things out in faith-filled intercession. He wanted his readers to understand the challenging processes. Many times, healing ministers don't share the entire story. The victories are real, but sometimes they only manifest after an intense spiritual fight.

9. It is interesting to witness the underlying dynamics of identity and sonship in this account. Allen's father died when he was young. Growing up as a sick, fatherless boy undoubtedly made a harsh imprint on his life. But Jesus made it clear that Allen was accepted.

10. Traveling during the mid-1800s, by horseback or wagon, was considerably slower and more difficult.

11. The "companion" Allen is referencing is likely his beloved wife Keziah.

12. Allen is "acting faith," moving forward with an expectation of receiving healing prior to it being fully displayed. This is a response that many within the Faith Cure Movement encouraged. Advocates wanted individuals to move forward like they were healed even when the cure did not appear to be manifest. A similar idea, drawn from Phoebe Palmer's (1807-1874) "altar theology," catalyzed the Wesleyan-Holiness Movement. A dedicated believer would, for example, "reckon themselves" "sanctified" by faith during a fervent revival meeting. Later faith cure advocates argued that the same "faith act" could apply to healing. The notion of "acting faith" shaped early Pentecostalism (1901-1946), the Salvation-Healing Revival (1946-1958), and the Word of Faith Movement (1968-present). See Heather Curtis, "'Acting Faith': Practices of Religious Healing in Late-Nineteenth-Century Protestantism," in *Practicing Protestants: Histories of the Christian Life in America*, ed. Laurie Maffly-Kipp, Leigh Schmidt, and Mark Valeri (Baltimore, MD: Johns Hopkins University Press, 2006), 137-158.

13. Allen continued to work at a poorhouse, taking care of the needy and destitute.

14. Dysentery is a severe intestinal infection that causes immense diarrhea and produces blood and mucus in the feces.

15. Allen drew understanding from James 1:2-4: "My brethren, count it all joy when you fall into various trials, knowing that the testing of your faith produces patience. But let patience have its perfect work, that you may be perfect and complete, lacking nothing." He saw sickness and other trials as an opportunity to actively test faith. After feeling he was unfaithful to God in his previous interchange, Allen wanted another chance to prove his unwavering trust in Jesus.

16. "Selectmen" was a term for the local government board of a New England town. These men oversaw the poorhouse.

17. Allen, rooted in a Wesleyan-Holiness theology, thought that everything in the Kingdom of God was directly tied to holiness

and purity. Without sanctification, there would be no works of power.

18. Allen is basically affirming the reality of the double-cure. Jesus' atoning blood not only saves a soul, but it also heals a body. Allen and other teachers from this era centered their teaching on Psalm 103:2-3: "Bless the Lord, O my soul, and forget not all his benefits: Who forgiveth all thine iniquities; who healeth all thy diseases."

19. Allen explains that he had to learn about faith and the realities of prayer through difficult personal trials. Under great duress, he prevailed.

20. By "fits," Allen is referencing seizures or severe convulsions. The woman may have had epilepsy.

21. An "almshouse" is another name for a "poorhouse." It was a facility for the poor or mentally challenged. Apparently, this was the facility where Allen worked.

22. Although Gross was not destitute or without family, he was being brought to the poorhouse for the convivence of friends and loved ones. It was considered an appropriate place to visit and engage with him before dying. Allen and the poorhouse, in this instance, were serving as a hospice.

23. Although identifying with Methodism and Holiness groups, Allen also associated with the Seventh Day Adventists. This group grew out of the Premillennial Millerite movement in the 1840s. Allen was attracted to their apocalyptic ethos, teachings on Old Testament dietary principles, and Sabbath-day worship. Ellen White, a key figure in Adventist circles wrote a book titled, *The Ministry of Healing* (1905). So, divine healing was practiced in some Adventist churches.

24. In this entry, Allen is reiterating the importance of faith. One must believe without seeing. Having confidence in God, before the act of healing, positions one for breakthrough.

25. Allen always emphasizes the prophetic leadings of God. Whenever he felt a strong assurance of a healing, he knew that it was done. In this case, he had not yet received any kind of guidance from the Holy Spirit. He would, however, receive a greater inundation of power as he continued.

26. He was raucous and vomiting.

27. Allen thought that what he was experiencing in this situation was a "blow-back." Sometimes, after driving out demons and making an advancement against the work of Satan, the wretched one would send demons and other vile things as an act of retaliation. Some healing practitioners thought that the devil would try to place on the intercessor the affliction that was originally on the one that was healed.

28. Prayer meetings or other spiritual gatherings were occasionally organized in Allen's home.

29. "Water-cure" and various hydropathy treatments gained popularity in the United States and Europe in the 1800s. Practitioners argued that water had the ability to cure a host of debilitating diseases. Allen did not believe in the validity of these treatments.

30. There is a supernatural power, a prophetic realization, a reality of active faith that Allen and his colleagues depended on. Without it, they were convinced that they were ineffective.

31. These men were experiencing, in their bold intercession, a tangible sense of the power of God.

32. Although the victory was assured, Allen had to press in a little more to get to the final outcome. Kingdom realities have to sometimes be appropriated.

33. Allen's remarkable healing and triumph of faith became a catalyst for other healing exploits.

34. "Consumption" was the common term for tuberculosis in the nineteenth and early twentieth centuries.

35. Again, Allen is referencing a tangible sense of the glory. It is a reality that he and the other intercessors directly encountered.

36. In the late nineteenth century, many became fascinated with spiritualism, which was made up of occult practices like communicating with the spirits of the dead. Allen rightly understood this as an unholy practice that was contrary to scripture. The people involved with this were being infested by demons.

37. By "excitement," Allen is referencing the unusual manifestations and outbursts caused by the demons.

38. Allen is referencing a special healing anointing—an infusion of power that enables miracles to happen.

39. Dorothea Trudel, in Switzerland, would often lay next to the severely diseased women who came to her healing home and pray for them all through the night. Both Trudel and Allen understood the value of this kind of prayer, particularly if the diseases involved demons.

40. Erysipelas is a painful and shiny light-red swelling of a defined area of the skin.

41. A poultice is a small cloth with plant or other form of medicinal material applied to the body to relieve soreness and inflammation.

42. Sometimes a disease that originates spiritually will move around in the body. The ache may, for example, move from the chest to the arm. An afflicting spirit often advances toward the external extremities—the arms, legs, or the head. It is unclear if this is what is happening in this account.

43. Rather than petitioning God for healing like Protestants have traditionally done, Allen and his associates utilized "commanding prayers," battling against the forces of darkness. This was the common pattern of intercession in the New Testament.

44. Allen understood the power of agreement when it came to healing prayer (Amos 3:3). It is difficult to effectively minister alongside someone who will not stand with you in faith and biblical understanding.

45. Allen and his colleague were trying to better their financial situation with the acquisition of the farm. But they were unsuccessful in this effort.

46. Allen believed that an individual's eyes could reveal a lot about what is going on in their spirit. This applied to deliverance and healing. He drew inspiration from Matthew 6:22: "Your eye is like a lamp that provides light for your body. When your eye is healthy, your whole body is filled with light."

47. In several of these stories, Allen and his colleagues have to deal with the reappearances of sickness. They found powerful ways to counteract the continuing works of darkness.

48. Allen is likely referring to renewing his commitment to faith healing. He did not turn away from his faith in Christ, he just let up on praying for others.

49. Dreams and visions were an important part of Allen's prayer life. He believed that he could receive prophetic leadings from God this way.

50. Sallow is an unhealthy yellow or pale brown color.

51. This is an example encountering the power of God in a form of "electricity" or some other kind of overpowering sensation.

52. A protracted meeting was usually a series of revival services or an extended camp meeting.

53. Ann Paine is arguing that the work healing is a defiance of nature's laws. Therefore, someone filled with impurities is in no position to counteract the natural order. Divine healing emerges out of a place of holiness.

54. A number of times in the healing testimonies, there are references to the movement of the power of God, likening it to electricity or some kind of energy.

55. The date of Ann Paine's testimony, 1866, suggests that much of the rest of this book was written in the late 1860s.

56. Prayer, again, was understood to be most appropriate, while under the anointing. Believers who were consecrated to God and under the unction of the Holy Spirit, were those who were positioned to effectively pray.

57. The matter of functional authority and coming into agreement with God was paramount. Allen and his associates believed that an unwillingness to align with Spirit-led leaders or the Bible, inhibits healing. They understood these matters to be a part of the outworking of the Kingdom rule of God. Permissions had to be obtained and agreements established.

58. Allen thought that it was important to pray with the parents before praying for the child.

59. All kinds of responses occur during healing prayer. There may be a sense of heat, intense trembling. Sometimes the recipients might feel strange sensations or even a brief increase of pain before things get better. It was not unusual for the recipients to scream or shout.

60. Unbelief can hinder healing. Allen needed those who were interceding with him to trust in the work of God.

61. Allen says that believers who have experienced breakthrough and been used as vessels of healing should document their

experiences. People need to hear about the wonderful works of God.

62. Allen began praying for the sick in 1846. So, the fact that he was referring to twenty years of ministry in this passage, suggests that this part of the book was written around 1866. Other teachings from Allen, represented in other works—including his pamphlet, "Satan Under Your Feet"—seem to reflect a more developed theology and prayer modality.

63. Fanaticism was a negative term that was synonymous with enthusiasm. The idea was that anyone who believed in healing was unreasonable and excessive. Allen and many of the early Faith Cure figures were widely criticized for their belief in the contemporary works of the Spirit.

64. Love Feasts were gatherings where Methodists from various regional churches would get together for a special communion service. They would drink from the cup, give it to the person sitting next to them, and speak a word of blessing or a prayer. Afterward the pattern would continue until the cup passed to every person. People would sometimes share the gospel and people would get saved. It was a deeply relational affair that was beloved in early American Methodism.

65. Allen believed that divine healing was a pivotal apostolic doctrine that was in the foundation of the original declaration of the gospel. To him, it was a significant part of biblical faith.

66. Ethan O. Allen appears to have had an apocalyptic worldview throughout his ministry. Moving away from the Postmillennial ethos of Methodism and the early Holiness Movement, he eagerly embraced premillennialism. This eschatology seems to align with Allen's dualism and spiritual warfare focus.

HEALING PIONEER

1. The Old Orchard Convention was one of the most popular gatherings for the Christian and Missionary Alliance, a prominent Holiness and healing fellowship. MacArthur reconnected with Allen when he moved out to California in 1893.

2. American Methodism was drastically changing in the mid-1800s. Growing affluence and education were causing many in the denomination to turn away from the older revivalistic fervor.

3. The "old commission," as Allen called it, was the decree that Jesus made over "all who believe" in Mark 16:17-18. The Lord commissioned his followers to heal the sick and operate in works of power.

4. The Schuylkill River was a polluted water source in the late 1800s. It ran from northwest to southeast in eastern Pennsylvania.

5. By "prayer calls," Sellew is referencing the healing missions and private outreaches that he would go on with Allen. When the old evangelist felt like he had a leading from God, he would visit people and pray for their healing.

6. A.B. Simpson was a gifted writer and the founder of the Christian and Missionary Alliance. He was one of the most prominent healing ministers in the late nineteenth century.

7. In this example, Allen describes the power of God very dynamically. It was like the flow of electricity. There are several passages in the Epistles that use the Greek words "energia" or "energeo" to describe the supernatural works of God (See 1 Cor. 12:4-6, 12:11; Gal. 3:5; Eph. 1:19, 3:7, 3:20, 4:16; Phil. 2:13, 3:21; Col. 1:29).

8. Sarah Ann Freeman Mix (1832-1884) was prominent African-American healer from Wolcott, Connecticut that Ethan Allen helped raise up. For more about her, see Sarah Ann Mix, *Faith Cures, and Answer to Prayer: The Life and Work of the First African American Healing Evangelist*, ed. Rosemary D. Gooden (Syracuse, New York: Syracuse University Press, 2001).

9. Mrs. Sarah G. Beck oversaw the Kemuel House, a healing home in Germantown, Pennsylvania loosely connected to the Christian and Missionary Alliance.

10. Michael (1834-1910) and Elizabeth Baxter (1837-1926) were the editors of the *Christian Herald* and were prominent leaders in the Keswick and Higher Life Movements. The couple helped William and Mary Boardman open the Bethshan Healing Home in London.

11. Isaac L. Hess was the superintendent of the Alliance Mission work under A.B. Simpson. He later traveled to China as a missionary, where he was extremely fruitful.

12. The term "inmate" is now associated with those in prison, but the term was also used for an individual confined to a hospital or psychiatric institution.

13. Carrie Judd Montgomery's testimony about Allen was from the mid-1920s. Since Allen had died close to twenty years before, she was not as clear on all her memories about him.

14. The House of Peace was a faith healing home that Carrie Judd Montgomery and her husband, George, founded in Beulah Heights, California.

15. Anna Cassel Reiff was not personally acquainted with Ethan Allen. This article, from the 1930s, was a compilation of a number of testimonies and reports from others. Please note that this essay has been edited.

DEATH OF PIONEER HEALER BY PRAYER

1. There is sharp disagreement among historians about the truth of this claim. It has not been confirmed whether Ethan Otis Allen is related to this notable revolutionary figure.

2. Over the last two decades of his life, Allen gained some measure of prominence in the Christian and Missionary Alliance. He spoke in some of the larger conventions and was discussed in popular periodicals.

3. The belief that healing is in the atonement was not commonly held in the 1840s. Otto Stockmayer (1838-1917) was the first to put this assertion into print in his work *Sickness and the Gospel* (1879). But Allen was undoubtedly a pioneer in this teaching.

4. Dorothea Trudel (1813-1862) established the Elim Institute, a healing home, in Männedorf, Switzerland. She began praying for the sick in the late 1840s and became noted for her compassion for the needy.

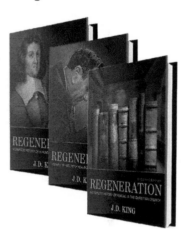

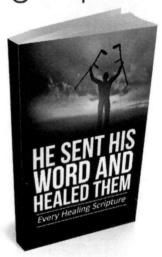

Also Available From Christos Publishing:

Why You've Been Duped Into Believing That The World Is Getting Worse

"For us Baby Boomer Christians who grew up on The Late Great Planet Earth, the future was deliciously and fascinatingly evil. J.D. King, in his latest book, asserts that we have been "duped" by this gloomy view of the future. Via numerous documented metrics, King shows that the influence of Christian values—and the growth of Christianity itself—is raising the quality of life around the globe."

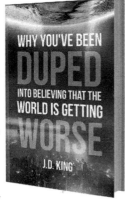

—JON MARK RUTHVEN, PhD.
Author of *On the Cessation of the Charismata* and *What's Wrong with Protestant Theology*

Find out more at TheResurgenceStore.com

Made in the USA
Columbia, SC
14 November 2022

10fcdce7-dcf8-417e-84b2-7ecd389972e5R02